How to Love Like
a Hot Chick

How to Love Like
a Hot Chick

The Girlfriend to Girlfriend Guide to Getting the Love You Deserve

Jodi Lipper & Cerina Vincent

COLLINS LIVING

An Imprint of HarperCollins *Publishers*

HarperCollins books may be purchased for educational, business, or sales promotional use. For information please write: Special Markets Department, HarperCollins Publishers, 10 East 53rd Street, New York, NY 10022.

FIRST EDITION

Designed by Reshma Chattaram Chamberlin

Library of Congress Cataloging-in-Publication Data

Lipper, Jodi.
    How to love like a hot chick : the girlfriend to girlfriend guide to getting the love you deserve / by Jodi Lipper & Cerina Vincent.
        p. cm.
    ISBN 978-0-06-170644-8
        1. Dating (Social customs) 2. Man-woman relationships. I. Vincent, Cerina. II. Title.
    HQ801.L493 2009
    646.7'7082—dc22

                                                    2008027728

09 10 11 12 13   OV/RRD   10 9 8 7 6 5 4 3 2 1

For Dan & Ben
With (what else?) love

Contents

Hot Chick *(definition)*: A confident woman. She knows what she wants and gets it. She is aware of her flaws, but she doesn't obsess over them and instead thinks that maybe (just maybe) they actually add to her unique beauty. She is passionate. She loves life. She is comfortable in her own skin and owns her sexuality, but uses it purely for good. She does not see other women as her enemy and competes only with herself to do her best at all times and to be her best at all times. She is forthright, honest, and disarmingly herself. She has fun and she is sexy, and you just want to be around her to soak up some of those good vibes. She isn't perfect, but she doesn't care because she is hot. And so are you.

Introduction

What Does It Mean to Love Like a Hot Chick?

THE FIRST THING WE WANT TO SAY TO YOU IS THAT YOU ARE A HOT CHICK. Somewhere between the bastard who never called after your fantastic first date and that old boyfriend whose head would do a complete one-eighty to check out any passing blond, you just forgot. Or maybe you never knew that you were hot. That's okay. We forgot for a while there ourselves. We spent way too much time being LSE♥1 around guys, dating the wrong ones, and thinking that we didn't deserve what we really wanted. To be honest, we weren't actually so sure what it was we even wanted! We were so busy trying to be perfect all the time that we lost sight of who we really were. On a quest to live up to somebody else's idea of beauty, we spent too much time at the gym and skipped social events to ensure

---

1. Any time you see one of these ♥, flip to the "Hot Lingo" section for the definition.

eight hours of beauty sleep every night. And when we somehow found ourselves on a date, we remained in our own heads the whole time, debating whether or not we should splurge on dessert and censoring ourselves to make sure that we always said the right thing. And you know what? That wasn't hot, and neither were we!

We woke up one day, though, and decided that enough was enough. We did a little experiment and decided to just tell ourselves that we were hot and that we were worthy of a fabulous man who was going to buy us pancakes and throw us against the wall (not necessarily in that order) and everything in between. And the weirdest thing happened: our lives literally changed overnight. The instant we decided that we were hot, everyone else started treating us like we were hot, too! Boys started coming out of the freaking woodwork—the kind of guys we always wanted but never believed existed.

Since then, we have spent a lot of time single, a *lot* of time dating, and (thank goodness) a lot of time being in love. And you know what? There is a lot of stress and crying and confusion that comes along with all three. Many of us think that all of that nonsense will be over once we find our proverbial Prince Charming, but the sad truth is that even the man of your dreams is gonna confound and annoy the crap out of you pretty damn often. But don't worry. We can't provide you with a man and we can't change the one you already have, but we are going to remind you of one very important thing that will transform your love life forever—that you are a Hot Chick.

We are going to get you out of your LSE♥ rut and teach you how to bring out the confident, sexy Hot Chick that is taking a nap right now inside of you. Whether you are single, dating, married, in a relationship, or are so confused that you don't know what the hell your status even is, we are going to help you laugh your way through all of the obstacles you will ever face in your love life. And we'll show you how to tackle them like the sexy, fabulous woman you deserve to be.

How to Love Like
a Hot Chick

Chapter 1

Love Yourself

BEFORE WE GET INTO THE NITTY-GRITTY OF LOVE AND
RELATIONSHIPS, WE WANT TO DEVOTE SOME TIME TO
YOU SINGLE LADIES. We think that the time a woman spends
being single is one of the most important periods in her life,
and we should all intentionally spend a while unattached.
However, we also know that being single has a downside, just
like everything else. We know that many of you view being
single as lonely and depressing. You wander around obsessing
over how to find someone, where to find someone, and why the
hell you can't find someone.

We know how badly you torture yourself over this, because we sure
did the same thing! We've had our fair share of casual boyfriends
and long-ass relationships, but we also spent a giant chunk of our
heyday♥ being incredibly single and perplexed. We sat around
watching *The Bachelor* and talking about how LSE♥ we felt, and

it took us a long time to realize that we were not only wasting our time, but that we were also sending that LSE♥ vibe out to the universe♥ and scaring guys off with it. We finally built up our confidence and told each other that we were Hot Chicks, and our single lives quickly got a lot more interesting.

Well, we don't want you to waste as much time as we did. If you've been depressed about being single, we want you to turn it around right now and start acting like the Hot Chick that you are. Whether you've never had a boyfriend or you're newly divorced from your high school sweetheart and single for the first time since you were fourteen, we can help you make the most of this solo time. We are going to point out all the positive things about being a party of one and show you exactly how to celebrate your life as a sexy, single Hot Chick!

Being Single Doesn't Suck

It's time to do a little ass kicking here. The first step to being a single Hot Chick is to rewire your brain. We know that society can make life hard for single women, but you absolutely have to stop letting this get to you, because it is total nonsense. Stop believing that being single is inherently a negative thing. Stop believing that there is something wrong with you just because you're single. And most important, stop believing that your life has to suck until you find Mr. Right! Being single can be fun and fulfilling, and if it sucks for you right now, it's probably because you're making it suck by believing that it should. The more you tell yourself that you won't be happy until you find a guy, the less happy you will be. And the more you walk around with a foonge face♥ about being single, the longer the universe♥ will keep you single to give you time to figure out how much fun it can be.

So do yourself a favor and flip the switch right now, ladies. Recognize that at this moment, you are single for a reason, and just decide to enjoy it for what it is. When you find yourself getting down, just force yourself to stop thinking about the negatives and focus on all of the cool things about being single. Stop counting how many weeks or months or years it's been since you've gone on a date or gotten laid, stop being jealous of other girls whose boyfriends buy them pretty things, stop feeling resentful every time another one of your friends gets engaged, and think about this: this is *your* time and there is so much that you can do with the freedom you have right now. You have so much power and passion and creativity in your hot little body, and this is the time to use it, not the time to be preoccupied with finding some guy (or girl, we don't discriminate).

If you want someone, fine. We get it. And that's totally okay. You're allowed to want someone. But you need to stop worrying that you won't ever find that person and stop picturing yourself ending up alone in a moldy basement surrounded by cats. Look at yourself. You are a Hot Chick! But if you constantly obsess and complain and feel LSE♥ about being single, then you are not acting like one. This can be a magical♥ time in your life; you just have to decide right now that it is going to be. The instant you stop thinking it's so shitty is the moment your entire life will change. It may sound cheesy, but the universe♥ listens to our thoughts. So squash those destructive fantasy sequences♥ featuring you as the cat lady, and force yourself to think about how much your life *doesn't* suck. We promise that change of mind-set will change everything.

Single Experiences

We want all of you Hot Chicks to live your single life to the fullest. This is your heyday♥, and it is very likely your only chance to do all of the crazy, spontaneous things that you have secret fantasy sequences♥ about doing. No more wasting time stressing out about the fact that you still have your maiden name. Instead, pour all of your energy into the following life-changing experiences that every single Hot Chick *must* have.

Single Experience #1: Travel by Yourself

It doesn't matter if it's a weekend lying by the pool or a summer hoeing weeds on a kibbutz in Israel. There is simply no better way to get to know yourself than to go away by yourself. Being in a new city where nobody has a preconceived notion about who you are or has any clue that you sucked your thumb until the fifth grade is possibly the most liberating feeling on the planet. It gives you a chance to create a new persona for yourself—and that is the person who you really want to be. So, instead of flying home to your mama the next time you have some days off, take yourself somewhere new and get to know a new and different version of you. Just make sure to bring a piece of her home with you.

Single Experience #2: Go on Vacation with Your Girlfriends

This may sound similar to number one, but it is actually a vastly different (yet equally important) experience for every single Hot Chick. Pick a fun place and call your girlfriends or sister or cousins or coworkers and plan a girly trip. And please don't say, "All of my friends are married and attached so they won't want to go on a trip with me." That is playing small♥. Trust us, your friends want a vacation away from their men, and that's totally healthy.

It doesn't have to be expensive either. You can all drive two hours away, stay overnight at a shitty hotel, and drink mudslides at TGI-Fridays. Or save your pennies and go to Hawaii or Puerto Rico, lie in the sun all day, and go dancing at night. Whatever you do, just take this opportunity to really bond with your girlfriends and get to know them on a different level. These trips will make for wonderful memories to look back on one day when your name is Grandma. Just remember to take lots of pictures to remind yourself how hot you were.

Single Experience #3: Live by Yourself

We know this may sound impossible, especially if you live in some crazy expensive city. But if you can swing it financially, we think it's really important to live by yourself at least once in your life. This is a huge step toward being truly independent. Think about how accomplished you'll feel after hanging curtains and setting mousetraps yourself. Plus, the value of having your own space to decorate the way you want, and in which to truly get to know yourself and figure out what you want out of life, cannot be overstated. At the very least, make this a goal that you want to accomplish at some point in your life, and we're sure you'll figure out how to make it happen.

Single Experience #4: Play Hostess

Throwing a party is not only a great accomplishment, but it's a perfect way to celebrate your new outlook on single life. Don't you dare be LSE⌄ for one second and worry that your party will be lame or that nobody will come. Instead, act like the Hot Chick that you are, pick any excuse for a party you can think of (your birthday, housewarming for your new pad, St. Patty's day, Cinco de Mayo, etc.), make some fun appetizers, buy a bunch of booze, and create a fun Evite. What better way to celebrate yourself than to share your home with the people you care about? Plus, you'll be giving your friends, family, and coworkers a chance to relax, blow off steam, and eat yummy food. It will make you feel good to make them feel good. And you never know—someone may bring someone who is fun to make out with!

Single Experience #5: Go to Movies by Yourself

If you have never done this, you have to start now. Take yourself on a date to the movies! This is a very Hot Chick thing to do because it takes confidence. It may seem scary at first, but you will feel like a total Hot Chick once you get into the habit of it. The trick is to not let yourself feel LSE♥ about sitting there alone. Treat yourself well: buy a small popcorn or some fun bulk candy and enjoy people watching (without judgment, of course). This is a good way to remind yourself that you're not banished to your house just because you're single. You are allowed to enjoy all of the little pleasures in life, and might actually enjoy them even more by yourself.

Single Experience #6: Spend Time with Your Family

Not to get all serious and shit, but no matter how old you are, your family is getting older, too. And none of us will live forever. As you are running around all single and happy, remember to set aside some quality time to spend with the fam. If you find yourself in a relationship, you'll have to start spending time with *his* family, and then time with your own family will be cut short because there just isn't ever enough time. We regret not spending more time with our grandma or bonding with our sister-in-law or visiting our favorite cousin or having heart to hearts with our brother. Before you go adding another family to the mix, make some time for your own.

Single Experience #7: Educate Yourself

Don't wait until you have a man to start becoming the woman you want to be. Start right now. Take classes at night and finally finish your degree, or learn Italian and then reward yourself with a trip to Italy, or take cooking classes at a culinary school or a random art history course at a local college. Indulge in all of the things you are passionate about and take the time to learn about them. This will make you forever a hotter Hot Chick, so study up!

Single Experience #8: Buy a Vibrator

With modern technology, there is literally no reason that you have to have a man in order to be sexually satisfied. Get your hot ass to the toy store or check out the fun Web sites that we link to off of our site. You can discreetly buy a fun new gadget and no one will be the wiser. This is absolutely something that every single Hot Chick must experience! It will keep you happier through your single days, prevent you from getting desperate, and help you learn exactly what gets your motor running so that one day you'll be able to teach a man how to do that.

Single Experience #9: Buy Nice Underwear

We promise that just sliding into silky panties or putting on a blood-red bra will make you feel sensual and alive, and every single woman deserves to feel that way! If the frilly stuff isn't your thing, there's plenty of stuff out there that's more practical but equally sexy. Put on some flirty boy shorts from Victoria's Secret's Pink collection and see how hot you feel just painting your toenails alone in your apartment. Or take one of Victoria's other secrets and indulge in some of her Sexy Little Things. You will feel so much hotter—and when you feel hotter, you act hotter, and when you act hotter, everyone will notice. Pretty soon, men will be fighting to get a look at your new purchases, and it will be up to you to decide whether or not they're worth it.

Single Experience #10: Have a One-Night Stand

Some of you may be morally opposed to this, and if that's the case, then obviously don't do it. For the rest of you, be warned that this can be a tough one, and there will most likely be some repercussions. You may accidentally get attached, or it may make you feel LSE♥ or guilty or slutty. However, this section is about once in a lifetime experiences, and this is a big one! So if it sounds like fun to you, there is no reason you can't experience this, at least once. Just be sure to always be safe, use a condom, and follow all of our one-night stand rules on page 149!

Single Pros

Even after having all of those wonderful single experiences, we know that sometimes it's still hard to shut out those negative, nasty thoughts about not having a partner. Here is a list of just a few of the fun, happy things about being single for you to reread any time you're having trouble staying positive.

Single Pro #1: Sleep Soundly

Most guys we know snore really freaking loudly and some of them think they're too manly to wear that awesome little Breathe Right strip. Lots of guys also toss and turn all night, and some of them lead with their elbows: we've woken up with a sharp elbow to the spine more times than we can count. Others take up the whole damn bed with their big manly selves, and still others sweat profusely all over your beautiful five hundred–thread count sheets, even in the dead of winter. Some men (gasp) do all of the above. Suffice it to say, enjoy your comfy bed while you can.

Single Pro #2: Solo Travel

Trips are another huge stressor on relationships. Most couples end up in huge blowouts over things like whether or not to get "bumped" onto the next flight to earn sky miles, whether or not to pay for the insurance on the rental car, directions, meal times, etc., etc., etc. You single Hot Chicks, on the other hand, can jump in a truck and head across the country or just take off whenever and wherever you want with nobody to answer to.

Single Pro #3: You Don't Have to Spend the Holidays with Someone Else's Weird Family

This needs no further explanation.

Single Pro #4: Money Saver

A lot of single girls don't realize this, but being in a relationship is expensive. There are just so many more obligations that suck extra cash down the drain, like his sister's baby shower, holiday gifts for his family, and more dinners out. For those of you who are hoping to find a guy who is going to pay for everything, let us remind you that it is 2009 and the economy sucks. Open a savings account now.

Single Pro #5: Gym Time

When you work full time and you have a man (and especially if you have kids), it becomes really hard to find time in the day just for you. Pretty soon, you're missing your nightly yoga class to have dinner with him and cutting your workouts short to rush home and take care of shit. We want you to appreciate the fact that you have your evenings or weekend mornings free to go to butt class ♥, and enjoy your "me time" while you have it.

Single Pro #6: Remote Control

Men seem to be pre-wired to not only hate everything we want to watch, but to also get unreasonably angry at us for wanting to watch reruns of *Sex and the City*. Honestly, if we hear, "You've *seen* that already," one more time, we might snap. Meanwhile, a re-airing of the same *Simpsons* episode he's seen five hundred times is somehow sacred. Enjoy singing along with *American Idol* or cheering for your favorite C-list celebs on *Dancing with the Stars* now, because one day you will most likely have to share. Gross.

Single Pro #7: No Breakups

Do we have to remind you how much better it is to be single than it is to be in the wrong relationship? Breakups can be nasty, heart-breaking, and really interrupt your life, especially if it's gone on for a while and you've mixed friends, left your favorite perfume at his house, and bonded with his sister. Just be glad to know that you won't have to go through this, at least for a while.

Single Pro #8: Fantasies Can Be Reality

This is the time for you to figure out exactly what you want, when you want it, and how you're gonna go get it. Nothing is holding you back right now! Since you're single, you can spend all the time you want deciding exactly what kind of man you want. Then you can build him from scratch and enjoy your life to the fullest until he comes. Fun! (See Chapter 2 on how to build a boyfriend!)

Single Pro #9: Test the Waters

We don't advocate sluttiness, but this is the time when you are allowed to sleep with anyone you want. Hot Chicks don't cheat, so if you're planning on getting married one day, you better get it out of your system now. At the very least, have an exciting enough heyday♥ that you'll be able to look back on and blush. Just use a condom (or several).

Single Pro #10: Get Some Kisses

You can make out with anyone you want, as long as he is single, too. This one really is harmless, so have fun and live it up!

Single Pro #11: Bathroom Bliss

Unless you have a male roommate, you are so fortunate to not have to share your bathroom with a boy. Seriously, their beard hairs stick to the bathroom sink like Krazy Glue, they will do things like knock your dental floss in the toilet and put it back in the medicine cabinet without telling you, and, sorry to be gross, they can make the bathroom smell really, really bad. Oh, and we swear they use our expensive eye creams and teeth whiteners when we're not around.

Single Pro #12: Girl Time
You have more time for fun girly projects, and admit it, you totally get off on making scrapbooks and bedazzling things and using a hot glue gun to decorate picture frames. It's really hard to find time to do all this stuff and have fun girly brunches and go shopping with your sister when you have to make time to hang out with your man, too.

Single Pro #13: Private Parts
This is the time to get to know your girly parts and figure out what you like, whether it's with a partner or by yourself! You can't be a Hot Chick if you don't know your body and feel totally comfortable in your own skin. Plus, we want you to truly *enjoy* being single. So shut your bedroom door and have fun.

Single Pro #14: No Bickering
Think about the fact that you don't have someone always watching you and complaining about how you didn't cap the seltzer tightly enough or how your thick, lustrous hair always gets caught in the drain. Relationships can be great, but none of them are perfect. And arguing about really dumb shit (which is totally normal and healthy, by the way) can be really, really annoying.

Single Pro #15: Food Freedom
The number one argument between every couple we know is over where the hell they should eat dinner. But you sexy single girls don't have to wait to eat until your man gets home at 8:30 and end up getting into a giant fight because you're so LBS♥. Nor do you have to listen to a diatribe about how you put too much

importance on food just because you want to eat dinner with your man every now and then. You can eat frozen yogurt for dinner whenever you feel like it without anyone thinking that you're pulling a Mary Kate ♥. Eat whatever and whenever you want! This is a highly underrated freedom.

Don't Get Lonely

Loneliness is quite possibly one of the worst feelings on the planet. There are times when we all feel like we have nobody to turn to, nobody to share small moments with, and nobody that even cares if we get out of bed in the morning. Even the most confident, busiest Hot Chicks on the planet feel a little blue from time to time, and it can be even worse for single Hot Chicks. Even if you're pursuing all of your passions and you're out every night with friends, sometimes it can suck not to have someone to cuddle up and giggle about ridiculous inside jokes with while dozing off to sleep. But there is no excuse to have a pity party just because you're single. We just want to tell you that we know it gets lonely sometimes, and that's okay.

First of all, please realize that feeling lonely, whether you're single or not, is extremely common. It is part of being human. And all of you single Hot Chicks should know that women in relationships get lonely, too. Sometimes it's even worse. There is nothing more terrible than feeling all alone when you actually have someone lying in the bed next to you or a houseful of children to keep you company. It can make you feel crazy, but you're not. All women, whether it's Angelina Jolie with Brad Pitt and five hundred cute babies or a single Hot Chick with no family who runs a farm by herself, all have the same womanly emotions and insecurities. This is sad, but it's also comforting, isn't it? You are not alone in feeling this way, which means that you are not alone. You have the power to take your loneliness and turn it into something positive. Look around your life and notice the acquaintances and coworkers who are probably lonely, too. Invite them out to a movie or over for coffee and keep surrounding yourself with people you can talk to.

It may not make you feel better right away, but sometimes being proactive is enough to make you feel more alive. Just do your best, don't pressure yourself to feel differently, and calmly wait for the blue feelings to fade into a bright, blushing pink.

We also want to make sure that you know the difference between loneliness and depression. If your bed feels cold and vacant and you hate coming home to a dark, empty apartment every night, or you long to have someone to watch *The Departed* with for the five thousandth time, then you are experiencing regular old loneliness. On the other hand, if you really don't want to get out of bed, you're crying all the time, you've lost your appetite, or you're abusing alcohol or some other drug, your loneliness may be more serious and you may be suffering from depression. In this case, we have to tell you what any good friend would tell you—you need to get help. You absolutely must take care of your precious heart and mind and delicate spirit. Go make an appointment, and then come back and keep reading.

And Don't Feel Sorry for Yourself

Even when you are feeling lonely, it is extremely important to present yourself to the world as a single Hot Chick. So many ladies move through life with giant foonge faces♥ and then wonder why they are not happy. Well, Hot Chicks, if you act like a sad sack, then that is exactly how the universe♥ is going to treat you. But if you act like a confident Hot Chick who embraces her life (even if she gets down from time to time), the universe♥ (and everyone else, for that matter) will see you that way, too. You really do have the power to change your life, but in order for something to change, you have to change something. Your attitude toward your life is the most powerful thing you have, so start by changing that first.

Trust us: we've been through this, too. We wasted years feeling depressed and angry and confused about our problems. But we woke up one day and realized that by focusing on the negative, we weren't seeing all of the beauty and abundance that was surrounding us. And as soon as we made a slight shift in attitude, everything changed. We realized that, sure, we had problems, but we also had a great life, a heyday♥ that we almost totally missed, and dozens of potential male lovers that we were being blind to. If you are beyond lonely and are single and mad about it and feeling really sorry for yourself, we want you to start focusing on positive things, not destructive fantasy sequences♥. The martini glass is half full, ladies, and it's a freaking martini glass, for crying out loud! Stop feeling sorry for yourself right now, because nobody else feels sorry for you. They don't see anything to feel sorry about, and neither should you.

Five Things a Hot Chick Never Does Just Because She Feels Sorry for Herself

As you stop feeling sorry for yourself, it's even more important to stop acting like you feel sorry for yourself with desperate, attention-getting moves. We all know girls like this, don't we? You have a couple of friends who act stupid and crazy just because they're jealous of what other people have and want to take it away from them. We really hope this girl isn't you, because if you have been involved in any of the bullshit below, then you have not been acting like a Hot Chick. Doing this stuff shows a severe need for attention and lack of concern over hurting people in order to get it. If you keep it up, it will only keep you stuck in a rut of loneliness and drama. So if you recognize yourself in any of this nonsense, stop it right now, and if this reminds you of a friend or two, run out right now and buy them a copy of this book.

Hot Chick No-no #1: Flirting with Attached Men
Hot Chicks, whether they are married, dating, or totally single, do not ever flirt with men who have girlfriends or rings on their fingers. Hot Chicks treat other women like Hot Chicks, and there is nothing more disrespectful to a woman than messing with her man. If you pull this shit, you are acting LSE♥ and nauseatingly desperate for attention. You may think it's harmless, but it rarely is. Men do not need to be tempted, okay? It may give you a little thrill, but it benefits absolutely no one to have that married guy thinking

about you while he's lying next to his wife at night. If you get off on that immature nonsense, then you are letting your desperation turn you into a nasty home wrecker. This goes for ex-boyfriends, too. So what if he used to be yours? He's not anymore, so leave him alone and let him move on. You are distracting him from the attention he should be giving to his current girlfriend, and you're distracting yourself from all of the other available guys out there.

If you don't give a shit about hurting other people, then let us remind you about a little thing called karma. You're also hurting yourself, ladies! If flirting with attached men is your thing, then you are in for a rude awakening when you finally decide to go monogamous. And if you make excuses like, "Well, his wife doesn't sleep with him," or, "His girlfriend treats him like shit," then you just sound like a really dumb girl. That stuff is his problem, not yours. Get your ass out of his business and focus on your own life! And please don't say that you actually want this attached man, or that you loooove him. You may think you do, but either he'll get a lot less interesting once his wife is out of the picture or you'll spend the rest of your life worrying about what other ladies he's flirting with (or both). So if you pursue him, you are only setting yourself up for more LSE♥ behavior down the road. Save yourself this drama and stop wasting your time on boys who are not for you.

Hot Chick No-no #2: Having Sex with People You Know You Shouldn't

If you're in a situation that is fraught with tons of drama and potentially bad consequences, it is not the time to lift your skirt. If you are doing this, it's probably because you feel incomplete or sorry for yourself, but by putting yourself in such situations, you are only making your life more dramatic, and not in a good way. This is also a good time to tell you not to use sex as a weapon. Go reread the Hot Chick definition and stop using sex as a way to assert your power over other people.

This part obviously includes sleeping with attached men like we just talked about, but there is another category of sex that you should never get involved in. You know exactly what situations we're referring to, ladies—we probably don't even have to tell you (but we will). We are talking about those of you who give your boss a blow job to make up for missing a deadline, sleep with your math professor to get an A, boink your brother's best friend to get back at your bro for pissing you off, or let a police officer feel you up to get out of a ticket. You are not going to end up feeling good about any of these situations, ladies, so don't put yourself in them!

Hot Chick No-no #3: Being a Bitch to Your Friend Because She Has a Man

This is something a lot of girls do when they're feeling jealous and sorry for themselves: they let those feelings come out as bitter, selfish, unloving behavior toward their friends. This first happened to us when we were in sixth grade, and we can't believe that it keeps happening so many years later. But there is always that one girl who gives her friends shit for having a boyfriend. Unless he really is bad for her, don't say crap like, "Well, he's a loser, so she shouldn't be spending so much time with him, anyway." It's none of your business, and you sound like a jealous two-year-old. If you really think that the guy she's dating is a dickhead, there's no better way to help her see that than by acting like a good friend. Give her space and be there for her when she figures it out. But the more jealous you act, the more she will pull away from you to snuggle up closer to her new man.

If this guy makes your friend happy, then you should be happy for her. When you fall in love with someone, all you want to see for a little while is him and his mattress. That's normal. So don't get mad at your best friend just because she met a guy and is spending more time cuddling in bed with him than eating frozen yogurt with you. You're not acting like a Hot Chick and you may lose a friend over it.

Hot Chick No-no #4: Complaining all the Freaking Time

If you like to talk about guys and dates and gossip and tell funny stories, that is fine. But it's not okay to constantly bitch and complain about how long it's been since you got some kisses or how everyone has a boyfriend except for you. It's okay if you want someone, and it's also okay to say that you want someone. Go ahead and tell the universe ♥. But there is a big difference between being clear about what you want and complaining about not having it. You are fine. You have everything you need and are ready to find a fabulous man to share it with. You do not need to carry on about how it's not fair, that all the guys you meet are dicks, etc. That just keeps you surrounded by negativity, which can be really hard to unravel. So the next time you're tempted to start a bitch-fest, just try saying out loud, "I'm fine, everything is great." Pretty soon, you will start feeling that way, too.

Hot Chick No-no #5: Pretending to Be a Lesbian

We want all women to find true love no matter what their sexual preference is, and we have absolutely nothing, zero, zilch against lesbians. However, what bugs us, and what we feel is a huge slap in the face to real lesbians, is when girls pretend to be gay in order to get attention from men. You know what we're talking about: straight chicks who will get drunk and make out with girls just to get a roar from the bar crowd, or who will flirt with a girl just to make a guy jealous. This is lame, attention-whore behavior, pure and simple.

It's also a bad idea to be that girl who says things like, "Guys are pricks; I'm a lesbian now!" Sorry, ladies, but one's sexuality does not change overnight. Coming out of the closet is a long journey of self-awareness, honesty, and truth for actual lesbians, and you are disrespecting them with this obnoxious flip-flopping. Instead, be true to yourself and what you actually want, and you will have a much easier time getting it.

Six Sticky Single Situations

We obviously think that being single can be really fun, but there are of course two sides to every coin, and there are some times when being single can be really sucky and inconvenient. These awkward social situations can make even the most confident Hot Chick feel like a big fat LSE♥ loser just for being single. Luckily (for you, not us), we've been through all of them and we can teach you some ways to get through these sticky single situations like the hot single woman that you are.

Sticky Single Situation #1: Solo Wedding Invites
What's a single girl to do when she gets invited to a wedding minus a plus one? Every time this happened to us in the past, we got really mad and offended. We assumed that the bride and groom thought we were so lame for being single that we didn't deserve a date and that this solo invitation was our punishment for being single. Well, guess what? It wasn't about us, and if this happens to you, it's not about you, either. When people are planning a wedding, they're not thinking about you or judging you. If anything, they're grateful that you don't have a man because it's saving them two hundred dollars! Weddings are expensive and delicate and complicated, and that guest list was crafted with as much care as a Fabergé egg. Some great aunt or neighbor probably got cut to make room for you, and they didn't want to sacrifice another relative so that you could bring your gay friend Jonny. Can you really blame them for that?

So just get over yourself and decide whether or not you want to go. If this couple is important to you, then going alone shouldn't stop you from being there. You are a Hot Chick! You can totally go hang out in a giant roomful of strangers and have a good time. Enjoy the opportunity to dress up, eat expensive food, and dance. Now, if you have a good reason for not wanting to go (like you secretly hate your coworker who is getting married), then just don't go. No biggie. But whatever you do, do not bring a date that wasn't invited, and please don't call the bride and ask if you can bring the guy you just started dating last week. That is just rude, selfish, and will seriously piss off the entire wedding party.

Sticky Single Situation #2: Family Opinions
We love our family, but they can really make us feel like crap sometimes. We have no idea why grandmothers and aunts and sometimes even mothers feel the need to say things like, "How come a pretty girl like you doesn't even have a boyfriend? Your cousin Betty just got engaged, and she's younger and dumber than you!" or "All I want is a great-grandchild but none of my grandchildren are even close to being married—poor me!"

We're pretty sure that your grandma has no clue how much these words hurt. After all, it's probably been a long time since she was single, and back then it was perfectly okay to put pressure on single ladies or think that there was something wrong with them. You need to understand that they are not actually trying to make you feel bad. They are just being old-fashioned and terrible communicators. They love you and they want to see you happy, and for some dumb reason they still believe that you need a man in order to be satisfied.

It's important that you try not to fight with them about this. You can't change ninety years of parochial thinking over one Christmas dinner, so don't even try. But show up to every family gathering prepared! Walk in smiling brilliantly and oozing all of that Hot Chick goodness that we know you have inside of you. And when they inevitably give you shit, simply say, "Right now, I am happy and busy and fulfilled and living a great single life, but the moment I find Mr. Right, you will be the first to know." How can they argue with that?

Sticky Single Situation #3: Couples' Nights

If you're single and you have a million other single girlfriends, it's really easy to have a fun, ridiculous heyday♥. But single life can be really challenging for those of us with a whole bunch of couples friends. Being a third or fifth or seventh wheel can make you feel lame and annoying and out of place. We've been there so many times, and we felt miserable at every brunch and movie and dinner party where we were the only single one. We felt like we were just interrupting their couple time with this pathetic pity date.

But now that we are the ones in couples, we realize how stupid it was for us to feel like a tagalong with our married friends. We love hanging out with our single friends, and in general we think it's fair to say that people who are in relationships still like their friends, no matter what their relationship status is. It can be really hard for a couple to find another couple where all four people genuinely like each other and enjoy spending time together. It's a whole lot easier for a couple to find one person like that, and if that person is you, then great. Stop feeling LSE♥ when you hang out with them. You're their friend and they like you, so just enjoy your friends and let them enjoy their time with you.

Sticky Single Situation #4: Holiday Parties

"The holidays" can be a depressing time of year for everyone.

There is just too much of everything—too much stress, too many social obligations, too many brownies everywhere, and too many gifts to buy. Then people get oddly sentimental about everything, which doesn't help matters. This can leave you feeling lonely and extra depressed if you don't have someone to hold your hand at all of the lame parties you have to attend. It may seem like it would all be a lot easier if only you had someone, and that even the office holiday party would be more fun if you could bring a date and make out in the corner all night, but this isn't necessarily true.

First of all, when you have a significant other, you will suddenly have twice as many gifts to buy and parties to attend. You know that if you drag someone to your office shindig, you're gonna have to buck up and go to his, too. And then you're gonna have to figure out what to buy him, his parents, his bratty sister, etc. Being in a relationship makes the holidays more stressful, not less. Plus, your fantasy sequence♥ boyfriend might actually hate going to obligatory parties with you, complain the whole time, and never shut up about how he thinks your boss secretly wants to bone you and all of your work friends are boring and lifeless.

So stop wishing you had a man around the holidays and start enjoying them like the Hot Chick that you are. Go to the parties that sound like fun and skip the ones that don't. Give yourself a break. You don't have to go to every single party you are invited to. And if you haven't been invited to as many parties as you should have, then throw one yourself! Remember that if you're sitting at home feeling sorry for yourself, then someone else in your life is probably feeling just as lonely. Invite over some friends or coworkers or start a new ice-skating tradition with your brother and his wife. Whatever you do, just allow yourself to enjoy this festive time of year instead of waiting for a man to come along and make it fun.

Sticky Single Situation #5: High School Reunions
We women put so much pressure on ourselves when our reunions come along. Whether it's our tenth, twentieth, or fiftieth reunion, we feel like we need to look perfect with a perfect job, a perfect life, and a perfect husband by our side. We have destructive fantasy sequences♥ about the entire cheerleading squad pointing and laughing when we walk in alone and the football team calling us a whale, but we are pretty sure that none of that is going to happen. If you really want to drop a few pounds, then go buy our last book, but if you think you need a man in order to go to your reunion, that is absolute nonsense.

Keep in mind that many married folks don't even bring their spouses to their reunions, and there is a very good reason for this. Reunions are awkward. Everyone barely recognizes each other and ends up engaging in meaningless chitchat in five-minute intervals. What outsider would want to be a part of that? And why would you want to add to your stress by having somebody else there who you need to take care of and make sure is having a good time? Go to your reunion with confidence, and when you get there, take your head out of your ass and look around. For some of these people, getting married and having babies is all they've accomplished since high school. There's absolutely nothing wrong with that, but remember when you start feeling LSE♥ that all those housewives are probably completely jealous of you. You are confident and sexy and have a sparkle in your eye that they know means you're having more fun than they are. Prove them right by enjoying this opportunity to look back on your past with fondness and appreciate where you are right now.

Sticky Single Situation #6: Valentine's Day

First of all, don't waste a single second feeling blue that you don't have someone to squeeze today. Valentine's Day is not just for couples. It is a time for everyone to express their love, and you should absolutely celebrate this holiday, too. If you are down in the dumps because you want a relationship, then start putting good, loving energy out into the universe♥, and we promise you will get it back. The quickest way to find love is to act loving, and Valentine's Day is the perfect time to start. Get cute little cards and Hershey's Kisses for everyone in your office or your apartment building, and send some to your parents and brothers and cousins. Sending out love only guarantees one thing—you'll get it in return, and giving is always better than receiving. (Well, maybe.)

Valentine's Day is also a great excuse to plan an extra fun girls' night. It doesn't have to be fancy or expensive or complicated. Just grab some girls and your gay best friend and get together to eat an entire red velvet cake while singing and dancing to Madonna's greatest hits. You can't possibly feel like anything's missing from your life when you're surrounded by such joy.

Another great way to celebrate Valentine's Day like a single Hot Chick is to put some time and effort into something that excites you. We're sure that you have some secret project that you've been dying to spend more time on. Haven't you been waiting for the right time to write a poem or practice the guitar or knit a new sweater? Valentine's Day is about passion, so take this opportunity to indulge in the things that you are passionate about, whatever they may be. You don't need a guy to feel like the fabulous, sexy creature that you are—you just need the things that you love.

Single and Sassy

Sure, many of us spend years trying to stop being single, but we know there are also a lot of you Hot Chicks who are living a sassy single life and loving every minute of it. It's not only fun to be single, but it is also very important! Women who go straight from one serious relationship to the next often lose sight of themselves or never give themselves a chance to find themselves. But when you spend time living alone supporting yourself, really, truly at peace with your sexy single status, you learn a lot about yourself. It helps you get closer in touch with your emotions and fears and desires when you don't have a man there to help you change every lightbulb and wipe away every tear.

So we want to give a giant shout-out to all you single gals who are in love with your single life and sick and tired of people trying to "fix" you by setting you up with a bunch of losers! We can completely relate to this. The entire time we were single, we were barraged with well-meaning idiots who constantly said things like, "Why don't you have a boyfriend? You're such a doll; it's so weird that you're single. Have you ever tried online dating? That might work for someone as busy as you are." We wanted to shout, "Leave us alone! There is nothing wrong with us! Let us enjoy our frozen yogurt at midnight and our Saturday morning yoga classes and our hours of watching *Trading Spaces* without your ignorant input in our lives!"

Now we want to shout at them for your sake, because we know that hearing all this bullshit is absolutely draining. But we want to take a second and remind you Hot Chicks that this is their problem, not yours. These people who are butting into your life obviously aren't living like Hot Chicks. They must be so bored and so understimulated with their own lives that they need to sit around and obsess about yours. So don't let them get to you. Don't you for a second believe that they're right and that there is something wrong with you since you're happy by yourself. Instead, tell them all to fuck off (but maybe not in those exact words). Don't buy into their bullshit! Don't try to make them feel better by going on a blind date with a cell-phone-salesman-slash-wannabe-rockstar when you know that you'd rather take six spinning classes back to back and then go on the Master Cleanse Diet than have one drink with him. Don't do it. And don't say, "Okay fine, give him my e-mail address." Then you might end up getting nine million annoying e-mails from some dude you don't give a crap about. Save your inbox space for the people you want to hear from, like Overstock.com.

You are a Hot Chick and this single time in your life is precious. Treat it as such. Don't let people get into your head and make you feel LSE♥ for not having a boy in your bed. They have no idea how cool you are, how strong you are, and how much better you will be in a relationship one day (if you want that) after taking so much time for yourself. Tune them out and enjoy your sexy single life like the sassy lady that you are.

Chapter 2

Get Ready for Love

EVEN THE MOST CONFIDENT, PRO-SINGLE HOT CHICKS ON THE PLANET CRAVE A LITTLE MALE ATTENTION ONCE IN A WHILE, AND THERE IS ABSOLUTELY NOTHING WRONG WITH THAT. Whether you are hoping to settle down or totally content staying single for the rest of your life, spending time with men is an important part of a fun, satisfying heyday ♥. It is essential for all of us to feel special and loved and cared about, regardless of our ultimate relationship goals. In order to survive, babies need hugs and kisses just as much as their mothers' milk, and while most of us give up our milk dependency at a young age, we never lose our need for affection. All Hot Chicks need to be touched every now and then and squeezed by someone other than our mothers, and we want you to know that you deserve all that positive love and attention.

So if you're ready to get noticed, we're gonna help you make it happen. But we don't want you wasting your time dating a bunch of losers, so in this chapter you are going to figure out exactly what you want in a man and precisely how to get it. We'll give you an action plan for getting the right kind of attention from the right kind of men, and after we're done with you they'll be falling right out of the sky. But before we get to them, we need to deal with *your* hot little ass. It's important to take a long, hard look in the mirror before you start dealing with anything else that's long and hard. Before you can meet the right man, you have to become the right woman, and we are going to help you find her.

You Deserve Love

No matter what your relationship history is, what bad things happened to you as a child, how old you are, or what size dress you wear, you deserve to have love in your life that makes you feel special and lucky and invigorated. You are a good person, you have a huge, full, loving heart, and you deserve to have someone awesome shower you with adoration.

Please don't think that this is easier for other women than it is for you. Don't tell yourself that it's uncomplicated for women who are thinner or younger or boobier, and that you are doomed to have a difficult time finding a date or a relationship. All women come from the same place (Venus, duh), and we all have the same girly parts, frustrating emotions, and crazy-making insecurities. We have all felt the same fear and anger and confusion about dating. Other than food, this is the one thing that all women torture themselves over, and we want the self-torment to stop.

No matter what obstacles you have faced in your life, never forget that there is someone out there who is dying to love you. If you haven't been loved in years or months or ever, you may think that it's simply because you aren't hot, but it has absolutely nothing to do with that. You are a Hot Chick and you should know that by now. However, sorry to say this, but it *is* your fault. We hate to build you up and then knock you right back down, but the only thing stopping you from getting what you want is *you*. The reason you cannot get a date or you only get asked out by the sleaziest guys on the planet is (get ready) . . . you are sending out a fucked up♥ vibe!

Vibes are those invisible things emanating from your body that either attract people to you or push them away. If you think this is bullshit, think about those women who you think aren't beautiful but who always have a swarm of boys around them: they are sending out confident, sexy Hot Chick vibes, and we are here to help you do the same. If you are sending out the wrong vibe, then you are most likely attracting the completely wrong guys (or none at all). The first step is to figure out exactly what kind of fucked up♥ vibe you are sending out so that you can fix it. Keep in mind that you can have just a tiny piece of one, or (God forbid) a combination of all of them. But it doesn't really matter how much of the wrong vibes you're sending. Any tiny amount will stop you from getting the love you deserve.

Ten Fucked Up♥ Vibes and How to Fix Them

The Awkward Vibe

Symptoms: Are you really fun and lively when you're with your friends and family but then suddenly get all weirdly quiet around guys? Do people say things to you like, "You just need to be yourself around men," or "You need to let the guys you date see the real you"? Do your friends set you up on dates and then report back, "He said you weren't the same as I described you"? If any of this rings a bell, then you are sending out a hard-core Awkward Vibe. You can be yourself around women and safe, undate-able men, but you let your LSE♥ get in the way with available guys. Guys pick up on awkwardness from a mile away, so it is very important to squash your Awkward Vibe stat!

Treatment: You are going to have to do a little acting at first. Before you go out, picture that fun, carefree woman you can be around the people you're comfortable with—the woman you want to be all the time. Think about what she would say to a potential suitor, how she would laugh seductively, flirt shamelessly, or even just project a quiet confidence. Then just tell yourself that you are playing that role for the night and in all of your interactions, pretend that you are her. Respond how she would respond, strike up conversations the way she would. Pretty soon, without thinking about it, you'll go from acting like her to just being her all the time. And then you'll really just be yourself.

The Baggage Vibe

Symptoms: When you meet a man, do you worry about telling him that you're divorced, that you just filed bankruptcy, or that your ex cheated on you with your best friend and then you tried to run him over with your Yukon? Well, by stressing out about these things, you are sending out a vibe that says, "I have a lot of baggage, and if you date me, be prepared for drama." The only guys that want to date drama are the ones who will end up making your life more dramatic. The other ones will run in the other direction (fast), so you have got to get rid of that Baggage Vibe, girls.

Treatment: We know this is asking a lot, but you have to come to terms with everything that happened in your past. You can't move on until you do that. If you dealt with a lot of serious shit, then props for coming out on the other side, but you still may need to go through counseling in order to totally heal yourself. If your baggage is not that heavy, then just stop feeling guilty and stop apologizing for it. So what if you failed in the past? Who hasn't? Guys don't expect you to be perfect; they just expect you to be honest and willing to learn from your mistakes. Show him that you have done so by speaking openly about your history (when the time is right) without being defensive or making a bigger deal out of it than it is. We bet he'll be impressed by how much you've triumphed over it.

The Crazy Vibe
Symptoms: Do you cry and/or pick a fight on the first date? Do you have road rage more than once a day? Have you ever faked a pregnancy? Are you intentionally dating the ex-boyfriend of the girl your ex-boyfriend is dating? Do you throw things, break dishes, or steal passwords? If you answered yes to any of the above, then we are very sorry to say it, but you are sending out a Crazy Vibe. Seriously, this has to stop. Any guy who's worth your time

does not want to date a crazy chick, so you have to stop acting like his worst nightmare.

Treatment: You thrive on drama and the only way to stop is for you to fully realize that you are a Hot Chick. You do not need a lot of crying and screaming to appear interesting, nor do you need to keep testing him to find out if he really cares about you. Just keep telling yourself that you don't need all that nonsense, and that you are a Hot Chick who deserves a guy who loves you for you. Just try it out and see how much cooler the guys you start attracting will be. We're sure you won't want to go back to your crazy days any time soon.

The Desperate Vibe

Symptoms: Have you planned your entire wedding and are just waiting for the groom to show up? Do you honestly feel worthless and incomplete without a man in your life? Do you think about your biological clock every day? Do you "fall in love" with pretty much every man who asks for your phone number? Do you flirt with your friends' husbands and boyfriends? Have you ever seriously considered getting pregnant just to keep a guy close to you? Are you always asking people to set you up with their friends, but no one really does? If this sounds like you, then we're very sorry but you are desperate and everybody knows it.

Treatment: Listen, it is totally okay to know what you want. You want to get married? You want to have babies before your eggs die? Cool, so do we. You don't have to apologize for any of this. What you need to do is be clear with the universe ♥ about what you want and then let it go. Tell yourself that you want it and you deserve it, but that you will survive if you don't ever get it. This will leave you free to enjoy your life while the universe♥ aligns things up perfectly to give you exactly what you want.

The "I Hate Men" Vibe

Symptoms: Did your sixth-grade boyfriend cheat on you and now you think all guys are untrustworthy? Do you hate sports bars with a passion that is a little bit too dramatic? Do you roll your eyes at guys in a bitchy way when they try to talk to you? Do you say things like, "I wish I were a lesbian," or "All men are scumbags"? Or have you ever actually said, "I hate men"? If so, you are sending out a strong I Hate Men Vibe, and it's no wonder you are scaring guys off. It's hard to love a hater.

Treatment: Wait, so *are* you a lesbian? It's fine if you are, but you should probably figure it out, because nobody likes a flip-flopper. If not, you probably just don't realize how similar men and women actually are. The first step is to work on getting to know the men in your life better. Drive across the country with your dad, go on vacation with your brother, or start having more heart to hearts with your male friends. Soon you'll see that men are just as vulnerable and LSE♥ as women, and quite often want the exact same things that we do. This will help you come off as more sympathetic and compassionate to men, which will attract them like bees to honey.

The "I'm Scared of Sex" Vibe

Symptoms: Have you never masturbated? Have you never had an orgasm? Are you secretly afraid that you're a bad kisser and/or might be bad in bed? Have you ever said things like, "Maybe I'm asexual," or "I can totally live without sex"? Does the idea of someone seeing you naked with the lights on scare you more than anything in the entire world? Yes? Then sorry, Hot Chick, but you are sending out an I'm Scared of Sex Vibe, and you will never be able to fall in love or have true intimacy if you keep holding back in this area.

Treatment: At the risk of it sounding like our advice for everything is "buy a vibrator," we have to tell you in this case to buy a vibrator. The minute you figure out how to get yourself off is the minute your antisex vibe will begin to fade. If you are still really scared of messing up in bed, download some porn or read a sex manual online. Just reading about what guys really like will help boost your confidence, make you heydayish♥, and put a sexy little smirk on your face that guys will notice from five hundred feet. (Note: If you are scared of sex because of some deep psychological issue or a history of abuse, please get help so that you can move on and get the love you deserve!)

The LSE♥ Vibe

Symptoms: Do you wonder why anyone would want to date you? Do you never even admit to your friends that you'd like to meet a man? Do you have a hard time ordering a drink at a bar? Do you not realize it when someone is flirting with you? Are the only men you flirt with always taken, like your friends' husbands and boyfriends? Do you skip parties and social events often because you get really nervous? These are all characteristics of extreme LSE♥, and if this sounds like you then you are keeping yourself single by sending out an LSE♥ Vibe.

Treatment: Stop saying mean things to yourself. Just stop it right now. The minute you catch yourself thinking something negative, just flip the switch. If you hear, "Why would he be flirting with me?" tell yourself, "Of course he is flirting with me. I am a Hot Chick and I have what he wants." If you think you are lying to yourself, then go ahead and lie. It doesn't matter what it takes to stop the mean, nasty, negative way you talk to yourself. Even though guys can't hear it, they can see it on your face.

The "My Friend Is Prettier than Me" Vibe

Symptoms: When you're out with your friend and guys approach you, do you assume that they are only interested in her? Do you constantly feel like your friend's wing woman? Do you joke with her about things like, "I'm the smart one and you're the pretty one"? Do you play small♥ around her? If this is you, then you are telling the universe♥ that your friend is prettier than you, and the more you do that, the more people will believe that she is prettier than you! You might as well just wear a giant T-shirt with a big red arrow on it that says, "She's prettier. Ask her out."

Treatment: Girl, you are totally fucking up♥! Quit comparing yourself to your friends. We are all uniquely beautiful in our own way, and we are not just saying that because it sounds nice. There are plenty of guys who totally won't be attracted to that pretty friend of yours. They'll think she's boring and will love your imperfections. That crooked tooth that you are really LSE♥ about will probably make someone fall in love with you. What? You have small boobs? Who cares? We know like nine hundred guys that love small-chested women. Plus, you have great lips, tiny feet, a good ass, and you're funny and smart and you can cook and sing! You can tell your friend that she is pretty (and you should), but don't you dare ever again say that she is prettier than you are. And the next time you two are out, start acting like the confident woman you wish you were. If you start acting like the hot one, very soon you will be.

The Slutty Vibe

Symptoms: Do you often sleep with guys and then don't hear from

them again until they want a blow job at 2:00 a.m.? Do you actually have sex with a guy at his place and then leave in the middle
of the night because you think it'll make him want you more? Do
you talk about other guys you've slept with when you're on a date?
Can you relate to any of the girls on *Paradise Hotel* in any way,
shape, or form? If so, then we really hope you are using condoms,
and we also want you to know that you're sending out a Slutty
Vibe. Guys want you purely for sex because that is what you are
subconsciously offering them. They actually think that you want
to be treated like a slut.

Treatment: Yes, you are allowed to enjoy sex, and we are by no
means judging, but you are reading this because you're not getting
the kind of attention that you want. You have to start acting like
the girl you want him to treat you like. If you want someone who
will bring you home to mama, start acting like a girl that he can
bring home to mama. You don't have to have sex with a guy in
order for him to like you, and you don't have to hold out to make
him like you, either! You have to simply stay true to what you
want and know that you deserve it.

The Unapproachable Vibe

Symptoms: Do people often tell you that they thought you were
bitchy when you first met? Do you hate talking to men you wouldn't
want to date? Do you have a hard time making eye contact? Do
you act intentionally rude to men you're not interested in just to
make sure they know that they don't have a chance? Would you
never consider dating someone who is slightly balding, is shorter
than six feet tall, or makes less than six figures a year? Are you
really quiet when you're out or when you're feeling LSE♥? If this
is you, then you are sending out an Unapproachable Vibe and we
bet we're not the first person to tell you this. Men are scared to

come within thirty feet of you because they're sure you'll either shoot them down or shit on them. You may not be doing it on purpose, but you have to stop being so unapproachable if you want a guy to ever get close enough for you to snag him.

Treatment: Being approachable is all about being friendly and fun and living in the moment. So what if you'd never dream of boning the guy sitting next to you at a wedding? We bet he can teach you something, and he might even have a friend who's perfect for you. Stop worrying that he's going to try to make out with you if you're nice to him. If that happens, you can deal with it, but that's no reason to be rude. Remember, men are just as LSE♥ as women, so it's gonna take a little bit of effort from you to start a conversation and/or keep one going. If you get out of your head and enjoy meaningless conversations for what they are, you'll be more likely to find yourself in one that's magic♥.

Good Vibrations

Now that you know exactly which vibes you need to stop sending out, you also have to focus on conveying the *right* ones. You know what kind of girl you don't want to be, and now we want you to work on becoming the Hot Chick you do want to be. If you just realized that you've been sending out a nasty combination of the Crazy and I'm Scared of Sex vibes, we don't want you to stress about it. Put it in the past and use your energy to start putting out good vibrations.

It is actually very easy to ensure that you're sending good vibrations. All you need to do is magnetize. Magnetizing is like having an intentional, focused fantasy sequence♥. The power of positive thinking is, well, powerful, so start picturing yourself as a new and improved Hot Chick. Right now (or right after you finish reading this paragraph), close your eyes and visualize in great detail the woman you want to be. Picture yourself being confident and sexy and empowered and happy. Picture yourself being this way at work, at home, at the gym, at parties, and on dates. Go back and reread our definition of a Hot Chick again and picture yourself oozing all of that delicious goodness.

Okay, while that picture is fresh in your mind, we want you to write it down. This may sound fruity, but just do it. Fill every inch of these pages with all of the good things about you, the things that already make you a Hot Chick, and everything else that you want to be, hope to change, or wish you were. Simply writing it down will help make it true. Once you take the time to write it down, all you have to do is refer back to this list any time you're feeling LSE♥.

If you're not sure what we're talking about, here's an example:

"I am smart, I am sexy, I am funny, and I totally deserve a hot, loving relationship. I am secure with myself, I am not jealous of other girls, and I have the power to get exactly what I want. I think dating can be fun, and I want to make it fun. I will not let my LSE♥ run my life . . ."

_____

_____

_____

_____

_____

_____

_____

_____

_____

_____

_____

_____

Gold Digger Guidance

If you ain't nothin' but a gold digger, we have a bone to pick with you. We try not to judge people, but it's really hard not to judge girls who believe that whoever dies with the most shiny stuff wins, or that marrying a rich man is a smart thing to do simply because he is rich. We just believe in plain old love. We believe that no girl should settle, sell herself short, or sell her soul for a four-karat canary diamond. We feel sorry for women who grew up having fantasy sequences♥ about men buying them shit instead of daydreams of romance. There is probably a piece of them that will never be truly happy and satisfied, and we think it's sad that they'd rather be dripping with pearls than experiencing deep intimacy.

Make no mistake—we want to relax on a pile of Betsey Johnson dresses as much as the next girl! But we'd rather have genuine love first. If something crazy happens and we suddenly get a million dollars and a Mercedes, then cool, but we'd honestly rather live with our beat up 1997 Jeep Cherokee with one window that won't roll down and no air conditioner if it means having someone we're so attracted to that we want to eat French fries off his butt. Being married to some rich, boring, stuffy man who will give us anything we want except for love, intimacy, and passion doesn't sound like very much fun at all.

But enough about us—if you are a gold digger, then you're really not a Hot Chick. You may be confident and smart, and you may waltz around in the prettiest things and live in the biggest house, but you are not using your womanly power for good. If you want a man who makes enough money so that you can stay home and have five hundred babies, that's fine. Flip to page 61 and write that on your Build a Boyfriend list. But if you marry for money and then bone the gardener or look down your nose at men with "normal" jobs, then you're a trifling friend indeed. Don't forget that it's possible to find both true love *and* financial success. And, excuse us, but why can't you make the money yourself? If you took all of the time and energy that you're putting into finding the richest guy and used it to start a business, get a better job, or invest in the stock market, we're pretty sure you'd end up a sugar mama shooing away male gold diggers by the dozen.

Build a Boyfriend Workshop

Okay, now that you are busy magnetizing and sending out the right vibes, you need to get more specific in order to get exactly what you want. Just like anything else you want in life (college, job, fit body, etc.), finding the right guy takes clarity, focus, and determination. Luckily, we have a strategy that works for everyone, whether you can't choose between all the men who are swarming around you, or you have absolutely no idea how to get a date or meet a man to begin with. Our Build a Boyfriend program is a specific form of magnetizing, and it's the perfect way to spell out to yourself and the universe♥ what type of love you deserve.

Before you go getting all skeptical on us, we want to tell you that we did this a few years ago and it totally worked. Back then, we were only getting attention from the wrong guys and could not find any of the right ones. We weren't looking for a husband or anything; we just wanted to start having more fun and date some guys we actually liked. But once we completed Build a Boyfriend, it was like a porthole opened up and a million Mr. Rights flooded out. And pretty soon, we met *the* Mr. Right! Since then, many of our girlfriends have completed the program, some who did want a husband and others who just wanted a fun new guy to make out with, and they have all gotten exactly what they wanted.

What you need to do is pull out a pen and write down, in extremely clear, minute detail, everything that you want in a man and in a relationship. You may need to sit down and think about it for a while before you start writing, because until you do this exercise, many of you may not know exactly what you want. You may have a vague idea, or know what you *don't* want (like guys with BMS♥), but we want you to be conscious of exactly what you are looking for, what will make you happy, and what kind of guy will make you feel like the Hot Chick that you are. Once you have a clear picture in your head, writing it down tells the universe♥ that you are a Hot Chick who knows what she wants and won't settle for anything less. So break out your favorite pen and let's get started!

Build a Boyfriend Workshop
Physical Characteristics (What My Dream Partner Looks Like)
Please don't just say "tall, dark, and handsome." Get creative, ladies! What do his hands look like? What does his body look like? (Picture yourself kissing him all over his body.) How tall is he? What color hair, eyes, and skin does he have? What does he smell like? How big is his package? Do you even care about the size of his package? Be honest. Does he have a hairy chest or does he wax? (To each her own, right?) You get the idea—now keep going. See how fun it is to fantasize about your dream guy! Remember, this is just for you, so go crazy and get kinky with it (if you want). There is no need to be shy!

Here is an example just in case you're still not sure what to do:
"My guy has wise, loving brown eyes that make me feel like I can trust him. He has sexy muscles but doesn't look like he spends all day at the gym. He smells like a real man, not like Axe Effect. My dude has a smile that melts my heart, and that makes other people happy and comfortable around him."

_____

_____

_____

Build a Boyfriend Workshop
Personality Traits (How My Man Acts)
This section is not just about how your dream man behaves, but also how he treats you. Is he jealous and possessive or does he love to show off your hot ass? Is he the life of the party, or is he quiet and reserved, and needs someone (you?) to draw him out of his shell? Is he open with his feelings or stoic and hard to read? Does he cry easily, or is he the strong silent type?

Example:
"My dude acts super silly with me, but in the rest of his life he is strong and confident and demands respect. He is a little bit over the top and is always the center of attention. He is always the one making everybody laugh and cracking jokes. He is really social and can talk to anyone."

_____

_____

_____

_____

_____

_____

_____

_____

Build a Boyfriend Workshop

Affection Style (How My Man Loves Me)

Next, describe how you love each other. Does he tell you you're beautiful? How often? Does he love on every inch of your body? Is he into PDA or more reserved in public? Also, be clear about how you show affection for him. Will he let you shower his face with kisses? Do you want to do that? Do you want to hold hands and go everywhere together and be best friends, or do you want a man who has his own thing going on and only has time to see you on weekends? How do you want to express your affection, love, and lust for him?

Example:

"My man showers me with compliments. He tells me I am beautiful every single day. When we're together, we're always touching. He does not shy away from PDA. He kisses me and holds my hand in front of his friends."

_____

_____

_____

_____

_____

_____

_____

_____

_____

_____

_____

_____

_____

_____

_____

_____

_____

_____

_____

_____

_____

Build a Boyfriend Workshop
Sexual Preferences (How We Do It)

How often do you want to have sex with him? What kind of sex? Afterward, does he like to hold you and cuddle, or does he turn on Conan and crack open a beer as soon as he gets his rocks off? Is he romantic? Will he throw you against the wall in the heat of passion, or will he make tender sweet love to you—or both? Don't be afraid to ask for everything you want. You deserve the exact type of guy that you wish existed but aren't so sure is out there. Well, he is, and this is your chance to remind the universe♥ that he's yours.

Example:
"My man is super passionate. He can't keep his hands off me. He doesn't hold back in the bedroom. He likes to talk dirty and say exactly what he's thinking. He buys me sexy lingerie and then tears it off of me . . ."

_____

_____

_____

_____

_____

_____

_____

Build a Boyfriend Workshop
Family Life (His, Mine, and Ours?)

What is his relationship with his family like? How would your family and he get along? And what if you end up together? Does he want kids? What kind of a dad will he be? What if he already has kids—is that cool?

Example:

"My man loves and respects his parents but is not too dependent on them! He could quote Curb Your Enthusiasm *with my dad and make lasagna with my mom. He definitely wants kids but not for at least five years. He will be a laid-back, openhearted dad who doesn't push his kids too hard or scare them."*

_____

_____

_____

_____

_____

_____

_____

_____

_____

_____

Build a Boyfriend Workshop

Career Path (What Does He Do?)

Is he a nine-to-fiver or more of an entrepreneurial type? Is he going to spend all his time at the office or rush home to see you? Does he make a lot of money? (Be honest—is that important to you?)

Example:

"My man pursues his passions but is also practical about making money. He may not have a ton of money right now, but he does have a long-term plan to be comfortable. His job won't take him away for long periods of time."

_____

_____

_____

_____

_____

_____

_____

_____

_____

_____

_____

_____

_____

_____

_____

_____

_____

_____

_____

_____

_____

_____

_____

_____

Build a Boyfriend Workshop
Passions and Hobbies (What Does He Like to Do?)

It's very important that you enjoy doing things together! Does he like to travel, or is he scared to leave his home state? Does he work out, or keep in shape by riding his bike to your house or chopping wood (Hot!)? Is he a morning person who'll drag you out of bed at 8:00 a.m. to take a yoga class, or a night owl who will keep you up late every night of the week?

Example:

"My man and I like to do active things together like ride our bikes or play tennis, but he also likes to watch football with the boys most weekends and doesn't get mad if I don't come! He likes to go out and have a few drinks on the weekends but rarely gets too drunk. He is really passionate about painting and spends most of his free time on that, which I think is really cool."

_____

_____

_____

_____

_____

_____

_____

Build a Boyfriend Workshop

Miscellaneous (What Did We Forget?)

Fill this space with anything else that's important to you. We're sure there's something! Does he support your career? Is he allergic to peanuts because you have a really random fetish? Go for it—this is your last chance to make sure you get everything you want.

_____

_____

_____

_____

_____

_____

_____

_____

_____

_____

_____

_____

_____

Now that you have explained in minute detail what your dream guy is like, all you have to do is sit back and enjoy your heyday♥. Feel free to refer back to it or go back and add things you forgot, like, "I want a man who puts the toilet seat up and doesn't dribble pee on my soft, white bathroom rug." But it's likely that you will never really need to look at it again. When you meet a guy, go on a second date with a guy, or ask for a guy's phone number, you will know in your heart if he is the one you just described. And when you meet a wrong guy, it will be super clear. A huge red flag♥ will go up. You'll feel a pain in your stomach and you'll get a headache. What is also cool about Build a Boyfriend is that you'll start to meet different kinds of guys. You'll start being attracted to something other than the "type" that you've always previously been drawn to. Everything you just wrote down will help you find the exact person you want, but he may be nothing like the person you always thought you'd end up with. There might be all sorts of fun surprises like that. So, for now you can trust that everything you want is in your heart and in your mind, and you can just have fun dating!

Chapter 3

Look for Love

NOW THAT YOU'VE SPENT SOME TIME LOVING BEING
SINGLE, MAGNETIZING, FIXING ALL OF YOUR CRAZY-ASS
PROBLEMS, AND BUILDING YOUR BOYFRIEND, YOU ARE
READY TO GO OUT ON THE PROWL AND START LOOK-
ING FOR LOVE. Fun! What's that? Did you just say that there
are no places to meet men or that all the good guys are already
taken? Well, that's all about to change, Hot Chicks. First of all,
you just fell in love with your boy on paper (or paper boy), and
now you know very specifically what you are looking for and what
will make you happy in love. And second, we are about to show
you that a million future dates are hiding right under your nose.
This is all going to come together so that pretty soon your phone
will be ringing off the hook (or vibrating off the desk, now that
phones don't come on hooks).

We know that looking for guys and finding dates can be a really grueling, frustrating process. Sometimes it seems impossible and pointless and utterly futile. But we want to help you enjoy this time and realize how much you are actually getting out of it. One day, you will look back on these times and realize how much you learned and laughed along the way. Plus, every misstep you take and tear you shed in the process of meeting men will serve to get you ready to find a wonderful, fulfilling love. So sit back, take a deep breath, and acknowledge the fact that this will be hard and frustrating at times, but also ridiculously fun at others. This is your time to open your eyes and see all of the abundance before you. The universe♥ has placed many male suitors on this planet for you to have fun with. We are going to help you recognize where they've been hiding and teach you how to make them yours.

Boys Are Everywhere (A.K.A. Twenty Awesome Places to Meet a Guy)

If you think that you have no opportunities in your life to meet new guys, think again. Even if you go to an all-girls' school all day and volunteer at a convent at night, there are still plenty of ways to meet men. In fact, once you start looking, you'll see that men are just like ants—you see one, and then another, and then suddenly you see a whole swarm of them building shit, eating crumbs, hiding in cracks, lined up against buildings, scurrying around looking for their queen, and trying to build a farm.

Okay, that was a little weird, but our point is that guys are all over the freaking place. You just can't see them for some reason, but we will help you realize just how many guys you pass each and every day. Sure, some may already be attached, some may be gay, and others may be total racist pricks, but whatever. Once you sift through all those dudes, there is still a plethora of penises waiting to greet you. All of the normal places you already go are crawling with guys who would kill to have a drink with you, a meal with you, or a meal *on* you. Here are a few places you've probably been ignoring guys for years. Next time, walk in with your Hot Chick good vibrations and say to yourself, "I am a Hot Chick!" It may sound cheesy, but you will instantly project a super-sexy confidence that no man can resist.

Boy Bonanza #1: The Bank

Stop sending text messages the next time you are waiting in line to cash a check and pay attention. Some of them may have rings on their fingers, but there are at least a few guys in the line that would love to make a deposit in you. (Sorry, we couldn't resist.)

Boy Bonanza #2: Bars

Some people think that you can't find a good relationship at a bar, but that is simply nonsense. Some of our best friends met their husbands in line to get a drink, so stop judging, grab a girlfriend or a sister or a coworker, and get your ass to happy hour! Sports bars are especially good, as long as you can get the guys' attention away from the game for five seconds. We think you can.

Boy Bonanza #3: Church/Synagogue

If you're religious, then the next time you stand up or get down on your knees to pray, take a moment to look around. Mr. Right might be in your pew. And even if he isn't "the one," at least you know Mom will approve.

Boy Bonanza #4: The Dry Cleaners

This is especially good if you are turned on by Wall Street types. The ones without housewives need help keeping those shirts stiff. Bring some silk lingerie to the cleaners after work and see if you can help in the stiffening department.

Boy Bonanza #5: Electronic Store

We're not suggesting that you buy a new flat screen just to get a date. They sell other things you might need at these male-infested stores, too, like cheap iPod covers, extension cords, and mouse pads. Don't forget to look past the customers to the staff, too, girls. Didn't you see *The 40-Year-Old Virgin*? Electronic store employees are always helpful, and you know what they say about a man who can program a VCR . . .

Boy Bonanza #6: Friends

Look at the people who are already in your life. Is there anyone you secretly want to date? If so, we'll help you ask them out in the next section. But also look at your friends' friends and friends of your friends' friends. You might know someone who knows someone who'd be perfect for you! So next time you have to go to a wedding or engagement party or birthday party or housewarming party, accept the invite and scope out the scene with all of your hot vibes.

Boy Bonanza #7: The Grocery Store

The produce section is always good, and you can tell a lot about a man by the way he sniffs a melon. But also check out the frozen food and cereal aisles. Single men eat a lot of fish sticks and Cap'n Crunch.

Boy Bonanza #8: The Gym

A gym membership is a worthy investment and not just so that you can take butt classes♥ and de-stress. It's also a great place to meet a man. We recommend skipping yoga class if you're on the market and heading straight to the weight room instead. It may be full of meatheads, but meatheads deserve love, too.

Boy Bonanza #9: Home Depot

Holy crap, there are so many of them! In every freaking aisle! All ages, races, shapes, and sizes. You may get a giant case of OWL Syndrome♥ because hardware stores are to women what Sephora is to a man—totally confusing and completely stressful. But there certainly are boys there, and they all know how to fix shit (Hot!). So why don't you randomly decide to paint your kitchen and go to the big HD for a can of yellow paint and someone to help you play with it?

Boy Bonanza #10: Jiffy Lube

Ladies, you need to get your oil and filter changed either every three months or three thousand miles. If it's been a while and you need an oil change in more ways than one, go spend a Sunday at Jiffy Lube. There will be at least a handful of guys in that dirty waiting room for you to choose from, and don't forget about those sweaty, grease-covered guys working hard under your hood. They deserve a chance to do that again.

Boy Bonanza #11: Jury Duty

Yeah, jury duty sucks ass, but stop complaining for a second and look around. They are legally required to have an equal number of men and women there. Lucky you! At least 25 percent of the men in your average courthouse would love to be handcuffed to your bedpost—even if they are innocent.

Boy Bonanza #12: Your Neighborhood

This may sound overly simplistic, but we actually know people who met just because they lived next door to each other. Humans are actually hardwired to be more attracted to people who live near them. Now, no home-wrecking please, but seriously, why not throw a party and invite all of your neighbors? Your future flame might live above you or below you, and that might end up being a very good position for him.

Boy Bonanza #13: The Park

Do you have a dog? Get out of your house and take it for a walk. Do you have cats? Well, then just go to the park, and walk around by yourself. You may step in a bunch of dog shit, or you may find a nice single man walking his dog or playing catch with his son. It's worth a shot, and at least you'll get some exercise.

Boy Bonanza #14: Pep Boys
If you don't have a car, we're pretty sure you still need a new windshield wiper, right? Well, you'll be needing one very soon because it's raining men at Pep Boys!

Boy Bonanza #15: The Post Office
The next time you are in line rolling your eyes at the old men who go up to the window to buy one-cent stamps, stop it and look around! Turn your foonge face♥ upside down. You never know, there might be a great single guy right behind you with a large package.

Boy Bonanza #16: Public Transportation
How romantic would it be to meet your man on the subway, the bus, or in the taxi line at the airport? We know it seems like something only Meg Ryan could pull off, but anything is possible. A couple we know actually met in their own cars while they were stopped in traffic. So the next time you're on the train, close the newspaper and open your heart.

Boy Bonanza #17: School
We know that some of you Hot Chicks are still wrinkle-free and cheating on your chemistry exams. Well, girls, you are lucky bitches. Unless you're at an all-girls' school, there should be a surplus of sacks surrounding you. Hang out in the library, the food court, or the weight room. If you send out the right Hot Chick vibes, pretty soon you'll have a male partner to study with. Just steer clear of the theater department when looking for love. Those boys are probably reading this book, too.

Boy Bonanza #18: Supercuts

Boys (especially single ones) love Supercuts. Those lucky bastards can get a haircut for fifteen dollars and still look hot. So the next time you need a trim, skip the fancy salon that's crawling with gay guys and go hang out at one of the cheap places.

Boy Bonanza #19: The Movie Store

Stop rolling your eyes. Not *everyone* has Netflix, and the movie store is a fantastic place to meet men. What's cool about this is that you can learn something from what movies a guy is carrying around. Do you want the one with *Jaws* and Red Vines, or the guy with *Lord of the Rings* and Goobers? Anyway, go rent a movie on a Saturday night, or at least go pretend that you're going to rent one. You may find someone to cuddle up and share popcorn with.

Boy Bonanza #20: Work

They say not to shit where you eat, but we don't know what either of those things has to do with dating (and we don't want to know). Anyway, your next ten dates might come right out of your office. Now, don't do anything stupid like try to blow the CEO or get some kisses from your assistant, but there might be a sweet single someone a few cubicles away who's lonely and looking for play.

How to Ask a Guy Out Like a Hot Chick

Now that you know where to find men, you Hot Chicks need to start asking them out. We are deep into the new millennium, which means that you can't sit at the soda fountain hoping that your poodle skirt is fluffy enough for Johnny to ask you to the sock hop. We know that some of you want Prince Charming to pick you up at seven, pay for everything, and then get down on one knee and surprise you with a diamond that's bigger than your face. Well, that doesn't really happen much anymore. Now that we women can vote, drive, wear cut-off jean shorts, have babies without men, and run for president, we can't sit back and wait for the phone to ring. And that is a good thing! You know what you want, and you also have the power to get it.

We know that this may seem really intimidating, and we're not saying that asking a guy out is the easiest thing in the world. But it is definitely not as hard as many girls make it out to be. If you've spent hours fixing your vibes, sending out the right ones, building your dream boyfriend, and magnetizing about yourself, why on earth would you just sit back and wait for that fantasy sequence♥ guy to ask for your digits? You're going to do all of that work and then just stop? How lazy of you! The more proactive you are, the more active your life will be. So, if that guy at the office makes you all heydayish♥, or you think you just met the father of your future children at your landlord's eighties costume party and you don't know how to make the first move, we can help. Here are five foolproof ways to ask a guy out, in order of difficulty.

Option #1: Be Suggestive

We don't mean to talk dirty and wear a low-cut shirt with a crazy cleavage-making bra, although that will surely get you some attention. We just want you to suggest something, anything. Guys can be kind of slow and LSE♥. Sometimes when you think you are being completely clear that you like a guy, he will have absolutely no idea. It's kind of funny, actually. We had this problem when we were single. We thought that we were being overly obvious that we liked a certain guy, but he had no clue—he didn't know *if* we liked him or *which one of us* liked him.

Anyway, this is about you. If you dig someone and he hasn't made the move yet, then you do it! And you don't have to make it a big production. Just be sly about it. Simply suggest something, casually, with grace and ease. You can just say, "Oh, you jog, too? Maybe we should go jogging sometime. I know a great park," or "We live in the same neighborhood? I should give you my number just in case you ever want to use the pool at my apartment complex." Or if this guy just caught your eye at the deli, tell him he should try that new brand of prosciutto. Don't be afraid to speak up and be chatty. Sometimes by merely suggesting something, you're opening the door for him to make a move. Oftentimes when you ask a guy to go jogging, he'll end up calling and asking you to lunch instead. Don't stress about it; just make your suggestion with confidence like a true Hot Chick.

Option #2: Be Generous

We want you to be coyly generous. For instance, if you're into a guy at a party, bring him a beer when you refill your vodka and soda. Or if you're at a bar, buy him a beer—that is always very much appreciated. If you work with this guy and you overhear him say that he's tired at your morning meeting, bring him back a latte after lunch. This works because when you give, you receive, and it is a great way to let this dude know that you like him. A warning, though—there is a fine line with this one. If you are *too* generous, you may come off as a creepy, stalker girl, so remember to keep these gifts small. Let's make an under five dollar rule here. That means no beer of the month club delivery or monogrammed Cartier watch. Just let him know he twitterpates♥ you by showering him with little bits of goodness, and hopefully he'll be inspired to come up with creative ways to make you feel good, too.

Option #3: Do a Group Thing

This one is good because there's less risk of rejection. Just invite the guy out with you and a group of friends. Remember that this is only a good idea if the group is a mix of men and women and it's clear to the guy that you are the one who is interested in him. He doesn't want to join you at your weekly *Sex and the City* brunch, nor do you want him showing up to a party wondering if maybe one of your friends is the one who wanted him there. To avoid this, say something like, "I would love to see you this weekend. Do you want to come out with me and my friends?" or "My friend Sam is having a party this weekend. Do you want to go with me?" This will make it clear that it is a date, albeit one with a security blanket.

Option #4: Be Creative

No more beating around the bush; if you're gonna ask a guy out, just ask him out! Finding a creative way to do it will make it even more special (and harder for him to say no). Do you know that this man is a huge Yankees fan? Then why don't you figure out how to get you two some tickets to a game, or at least ask him if he'd like to go watch the game with you at that new sports bar in your neighborhood? If you know that he's an art nerd, ask him to go with you to a new exhibit at a local museum. The trick is to make it personal so that he knows you put thought into asking him out. It'll be pretty hard for him to say no to that, right?

If you're nervous about actually asking, just keep it simple and clear. Just walk up to him or call him up and say, "Hey, Jay, do you want to go to Bubba's on Sunday to watch the Yankee game with me?" or "Hey, I know you're a big Jasper Johns fan. Do you want to check out that Met exhibit this weekend?" Just do it! He will be so flattered and honored to be asked out by a Hot Chick like you. And if he's not, then he probably has BMS♥ or some other horrible affliction, so you don't want him anyway.

Option #5: Be Courageous

This is the option where you just go balls out. No tiptoeing around on this one, just good old-fashioned honesty. There are a million ways to go about this. You can try, "Yo, I like you and I'm not gonna sit around waiting for you to make the first move. You want to grab some dinner tonight?" or if you have a motherly urge to feed him, try, "Not sure what you're doing this weekend, but if you want a home-cooked meal, I make a mean meat sauce." If you just met him at Blockbuster and he's holding a DVD of *Transformers*, you could say, "That movie sucks. Wanna go see a real movie together?" If you just want to sleep with this guy, then the best thing you can say is, "You can come over and do some laundry with me on Sunday afternoon if you want." We're not sure why, but men always seem to know that laundry equals sex.

Anyway, it takes guts to stop hinting around and actually say one of these things, but we strongly encourage you to try it. There is no room for LSE♥ here, girls. You just need to know that you're a Hot Chick and that you deserve to get exactly what you want.

Dating in Cyberspace

If you haven't found anyone interesting in regular life, then it's time to get your hot ass online. The very same Internet that wastes so much of our time and is killing our eyesight is also helping many people get the love they deserve. We know oodles of Hot Chicks who have found true love on a Web page. So if you want a relationship or you want to start dating more and you haven't tried the online thing, then you have no one to blame for your boring life but yourself. Dating sites are like a freaking Victoria's Secret catalog, except that instead of any shape, size, or color bra, you can get any shape, size, or color man! And a lot of them will do even more than just hold your boobs. There are hundreds of thousands of men online looking for love, so if you are knocking it and haven't tried it, then you need to shut up and try it. Don't you dare think that online dating is beneath you! We know actresses, actual *celebrities*, who have met their fiancés online. Seriously, we don't just make this stuff up. There is absolutely nothing shameful about online dating.

Yes, of course, there are some creepy dudes online, but don't be scared that you're going to end up on a date with a child-molesting polygamist who will sleep with you once and then steal your credit card numbers. You've fixed your vibes and you know what you want, so it is now pretty much impossible for you to even be attracted to such scum. Just follow our online do's and don'ts and have fun boy shopping!

Online Do's

Do Research

Online dating can be a bit of an investment, so don't just sign up for eHarmony because their commercials make you cry. Read about all of the different dating sites and find the one that suits you best. For example, if you're looking for an orthodontist from Jersey, try J-Date; if you want a hipster guitarist from Brooklyn who's a little bit kinky, try Nerve; and if you're into nondescript Wall Street types, you might find your match on Match.com!

Do Be Picky

Treat meeting guys online the same way you treat meeting guys at a bar. You wouldn't go out with just any sloppy drunk dude who winks at you. (At least, we hope not!) If you go on a date with every guy online who asks, you will soon develop such a giant case of OWL Syndrome♥ that you'll probably get burned out on the whole online thing before you even give it a proper chance. Be selective and pay attention to your ultra-important Hot Chick intuition. There should at least be something about him that piques your interest for him to deserve your time and attention.

Do Play It Safe

Not to scare you, but you actually can't be 100 percent certain that a guy online is who he says he is. Again, intuition is key, but you should also follow these rules: First, always meet in a public, safe place. If he suggests meeting at a sketchy park after dark, go ahead and suggest an alternative. Second, always tell someone where you are meeting and who you are meeting, just on the offchance that he happens to be a criminal with a cage in his basement.

Do Be Honest

You are a Hot Chick, and there is absolutely no need to lie about your age, race, size, or career. You don't want to get caught in a lie on your first date. You also don't want to see a look of disappointment in his eyes when you're not the 5'10", 105-pound supermodel you claimed to be. He'd probably prefer the real you, anyway, so give yourself a chance to make a good impression.

Do Make the First Move

There are so many people online that it can be totally confusing and overwhelming for everyone. So if you see someone who catches your eye, don't you dare click off the screen and hope that he notices you, too! You may not even come up in his "search" for some random reason. This is way easier than asking a guy out in person, and you have absolutely nothing to lose. Just send him a quick e-mail or a "wink" or whatever and say something really simple like, "You look cute," or "Hey, you caught my eye." And if he never responds, then who the hell cares? What did you lose—a "point"? So what? If you're so LSE♥ that this actually makes you feel bad, then just tell yourself that he probably got back together with his ex-girlfriend right after completing his profile.

Online Don'ts

Don't Be a Cyber Whore

Please don't be so desperate and narcissistic that you have to be on every single site just so that every single guy has the pleasure of looking at you. Don't confuse the universe♥ by telling it that you will date anyone from any site. Plus, do you really have time to check seventeen profiles? If you do, then you're probably about to lose your job, so start putting some more time into other areas of your life.

Don't Be a Tease

Ladies, do not let the anonymity of the Internet turn you into a flirty little sex kitten who writes sassy seductive e-mails and sends nude photos but then freezes up when the recipient of those sexy e-mails finally asks to meet you face to face. Have some respect for yourself, ladies; you don't need to pretend to be some porn star to get attention from a man. Show some respect for him, too, and stop leading him on. Work at being genuine about your sexuality instead, and if you can't walk the walk . . . just shut your mouth (or turn off your BlackBerry).

Don't Be Too Picky
Yes, we already told you not to date every guy online who asks, but you can't be too picky either. So if you're gonna go fishing, don't just catch them to throw them back! If you've already hooked them, then why not just give them a taste? It's a waste of time, money, and energy if you're just going to browse. It's like buying an expensive pair of heels and then never wearing them because you're afraid they may give you a blister. If you don't give them a chance, how will you know if they fit just right? Again, use your intuition, and if you're not 100 percent sure that you're not into him, why not give him one chance?

Don't Get Your Feelings Hurt
This is not just dating, ladies, it is online dating, which can be hugely impersonal. So don't take things personally. So what if you're not getting flooded with as many e-mails as you'd like? Then start making the first move. And who cares if some of those guys ignore you completely? Maybe they have wives and babies and are just online doing research for a book. Our point is simply that there is no reason to cry over a guy you've never met just because he seemed cool on a Web page. Please don't give the Internet that much power.

Don't Obsess
We are happy that you are committed to looking for love, but please do not make a career out of online dating. This is merely a

tool to help you meet men that you might not normally have the chance to meet. This should not occupy every minute of your life, and you should not shut down and stop meeting men in regular life, too. Keep those hot vibes flowing all day long and go on dates with a mix of people you meet at the mall, at the market, online, and everywhere else. We want you to use this tool for its purpose, but remember to power down your iBook once in a while and get out into the world. Too much surfing and you might just drown.

Don't E-mail Excessively

Of course e-mail exchanges are necessary when you're online dating, but please do not turn into an e-mail pal through drawn-out e-mails back and forth that are approximately the length of a memoir. He is not your diary, so don't treat him like it. Correspond just long enough to determine if there is any shred of potential between you, and then decide whether or not you want to get to know him face to face. And please don't pour your heart out to him for months and then disappear the minute he asks you out. Remember that you're online to meet a guy, not to avoid meeting one.

Chapter 4

Find Your Love

NOW THAT YOU KNOW HOW TO FIND DATES, IT'S TIME
TO ACTUALLY GO ON DATES. Yikes. Dating can be totally
nerve-racking and stressful, but if you can set your LSE♥ aside
and live in the moment, we'll show you how your dates can be really
fun and magical♥. The time you spend dating is the time to let your
hair down, kick your heels up, and enjoy your heyday♥ to its absolute
fullest. And we are going to walk you step by step though the intimidating dating process and help you have fun along the way. Just relax
and trust that the universe♥ will deliver good things to you as you go
out, create memories, and take pleasure in the process.

It doesn't matter if you're a senior in high school or a senior cit-
izen dating can be equally scary and fun for all of us. Just remember that going on dates is the first step to getting the love you
deserve, so we want you to relish this exhilarating process. Strap
on those strappy sandals, girls—we're going dating!

What Do You Want?

Since you've already completed the Build a Boyfriend program, you know exactly what you want *in* a guy, but you may not know exactly what you want *from* a guy. Before you embark on the grueling dating game, you need to know what your intentions are, because if you don't know what you want, it is very hard to get it. Think about it this way—when you're craving chocolate cake but don't put any effort into satisfying your chocolaty desires and end up eating a bunch of crap like Tootsie Rolls, sugar-free hot chocolate, and mini Snickers bars, how do you end up feeling? You feel like crap and you're still craving chocolate cake, right? Anyway, it's the exact same thing with dating. Knowing what you want before you go out looking for it makes it far easier to get, so you need to decide right now what you really want out of dating.

We've broken this down into three categories, and most of you will fall into one of them. Read through and decide which girl you are, and keep that in mind the whole time you are dating. This will help you get exactly what your hot little heart desires.

Pretty and Prowling
(You Are Dating Just to Date)

Do you just want to have a fun heyday♥ without the pressure of commitment? Are you young and not ready to settle down or divorced and not ready to settle down *again*, but you want some fun male attention? Do you just feel like sleeping around—safely, of course? (Sorry, Mom and Dad!) If you are dating just to date, then that is awesome! Just be very clear about that so you don't get caught up in something that demands more time and energy than you are willing to give.

Beckoning a Boyfriend
(You Are Dating to Find a Relationship)

Do you know that you don't necessarily want to get married right now, but you'd like to enjoy all of the ups and downs of being in a relationship? Do you want someone to go on trips with but who will also bang you and then have coffee with you on any boring Tuesday? If this is you, then you need to know it before you start the dating process. A man who is good enough to go on two dates with is not necessarily good enough to be your boyfriend, so be clear and enjoy the process of finding him!

Waiting to Wed
(You Are Dating to Find a Husband)

Is your biological clock ticking or are you tired of being a bridesmaid and just dying for your turn to walk down the aisle? Or are you just sick and tired of hanging out at bars and you're ready to find a man who will curl up with you to watch every episode of *Dancing with the Stars*? Or seriously, are you ready to find the one, fall madly in love, tie the knot, buy a house, and have a million babies? If this is you, then yay! We are so happy that you are being honest about what you want. Just keep this in mind while you are dating and we promise that you will end up with the love that you deserve.

First Date Freak-outs

A lot of girls get really stressed out about first dates. You don't even know this guy. It might end up being a giant waste of your time, or you might end up falling head over heels, which can be even scarier. Well, we want to remind you of something—you shouldn't stress out over a first date precisely *because* you don't know this guy, and therefore you have absolutely nothing to lose. Sure, it might end up being really awkward, but we're pretty sure you've been through worse things than that. So who cares if you don't find the perfect outfit or you choke on a chicken bone or spill red wine on your white blouse? And so what if you can't manage to fill every awkward silence with brilliantly funny anecdotes about your unbelievably impressive life? You are a Hot Chick and you have absolutely nothing to be afraid of. Don't play small♥; just be yourself and give him the opportunity to get to know you a little bit. That's all a first date needs to be about.

Of course, even bearing that in mind, you may end up in a few prickly situations, so here is our list of things that might freak you out about a first date, as well as simple ways of coping.

First Date Freak-out #1: You Don't Know What the Hell to Wear and Suddenly Hate Every Single Thing in Your Closet
Okay, relax there, Hot Chicks. You simply need to wear something that you feel good in—anything that you feel good in. Don't try too hard to create the perfect ensemble. It will end up looking too fussy and put together. Just think about where you are going and dress accordingly, but always keep it simple. So if you're going to a fancy-schmancy restaurant, wear your favorite

skirt with your favorite top or a basic black dress. If you're going to a dive bar, then wear your magic♥ jeans and the same top you would have worn with the skirt. Then have fun accessorizing— put on a pretty pair of earrings and a pair of boots or heels that make you feel sexy. Even if you are LSE♥ about your body, you can enjoy catching his eye with a sparkly necklace that flatters your collarbone.

Whatever you do, do not try to squeeze into jeans that are a half size too small or your favorite black dress from twenty years ago. You don't need to be wasting energy trying to suck it in when you should be listening to what he's saying. And if you really don't have any clothes that flatter your body, go out right now and buy one skirt, shirt, black dress, and pair of jeans that fit you well and flatter your favorite body parts. That's all you need and this investment will surely pay off on many dates to come.

First Date Freak-out #2: You Don't Know What to Eat or Drink
Do not stress out about this. If you are at dinner feeling guilty about going off your diet, you are not living in the moment and paying attention to what's important—like whether or not you two have chemistry or if this guy deserves a second date with you. If you end up seriously dating this guy, you are going to be eating in front of him all of the time, so you better start being yourself now. You don't want the first time he sees you mow down to be on your wedding night. Most guys actually like women who eat real food, so if your date encourages you to order a Diet Coke with a side salad, that is a giant red flag♥. Men assume that the way you eat is similar to how you are in bed, so you better hope this guy appreciates your appetite. Order what you are craving and enjoy every delicious bite of it. Do not play small♥ and apologize for eating. Plus, if you order a plate of steamed veggies at an Italian

restaurant, you're only setting yourself up to order Pizza Hut later when you're starving at 2 a.m.

As for drinks, if one alcoholic beverage or two will take the edge off your nerves and lubricate conversation, then we say cheers to that. But know yourself. If martinis make you say stupid shit, then order a vodka and soda and nurse it like Florence Nightingale. If beer makes you feel full and bloated, then you can enjoy a glass of merlot instead. But please don't think you have to impress your date by matching him round for round in tequila shots or Irish Car Bombs. Stay safe and conscious, but don't be super lame, either. If you don't want to drink, that's fine, but don't make him feel like an asshole if he wants to sip a whiskey neat. Find the balance and you'll both enjoy yourselves.

First Date Freak-out #3: He Wants You to Pick the Time and Place

Well, we don't love guys who refuse to take control because we think that bodes poorly for him in other arenas. But let's give him the benefit of the doubt. Maybe he's putting it in your hands to make sure that your date is convenient and comfortable for you, so you might as well use that to your advantage. We think that a first date should preferably take place on a weekday evening. This eliminates the pressure of a Saturday night date. We recommend meeting for a drink at 7 p.m. on a Wednesday or Thursday. This is perfect because you can suddenly have "dinner plans" at 8 in case you hate him, but you can just as easily continue the date and grab some food together if things are going well.

As for selecting a place, keep it simple. Suggest a neighborhood bar where you know you'll get good service but a giant group of your friends won't already be in the corner booth. Don't pick a super-swanky place to try and impress him. That might make him think that you want to be wined and dined to an intimidating degree. But also don't choose a dive bar with peanut shells on the floor just so that you seem more down to earth. Use this as another opportunity to let him get to know you, and pick a place that reflects your true personality.

First Date Freak-out #4: You Hate Him

No matter how much you hate someone, you can learn something from going on a date with him. So unless he is completely offensive, we think you should be cordial and honest and use a bad date as an opportunity to clarify exactly what you do not want in a man. Sometimes after you complete Build a Boyfriend, the universe♥ will send you a bunch of wrong guys as a test. Just relax, take it for what it is, and get as much out of it as possible. You can always go home and add to your list, "I want someone who does not stare at me strangely and silently mouth the words I am saying when I talk."

The chance that you might hate him is a really good reason to make first dates short—like a drink that could lead to dinner but doesn't have to. That way, if he's a nice guy but you have zero chemistry, after one drink you can say something like, "I think I'm going to call it a night." Easy. If he ends up being a total prick and he pushes you when you say this, then you can add, "Sorry, but it's not going to work" and get up out of there. In this case, we're very sorry that you wasted time straightening your hair for such a dickhead, but don't let him suck any more of your energy by arguing with him. That will only make it worse. Just get your hot ass home as quickly as possible before he tries to grab it with his slimy hand.

First Date Freak-out #5: You Looooove Him

If your first date is going well, then relax and enjoy every second of it. Don't think too far ahead and stress out about if he's gonna ask you on a second date or if you're gonna get some kisses. Just be in the moment, but make sure to let him know that you're into him. Look him in the eye and make sure you are sending him vibes that say, "Dude, I kind of like you!" Or if you are brave, you can actually say, "Dude, I kind of like you!" Just don't tell him that you think you are falling in love with him or have a vocal fantasy sequence♥ about what your babies will look like.

At the end of the night, make sure that he knows you want to see him again by suggesting it yourself. Guys are dumb sometimes, so tell him, "I'd love to do this again sometime!" You have nothing to lose by being honest. However, if you do this and he gets weirdly quiet or if he actually tells you that he doesn't want to see you again, please don't worry, and please don't cry. Honestly, he did you a favor, and now you don't have to waste any more of your precious heyday♥ on this fool who does not deserve your love. We promise he's not the one, so move on as quickly as possible.

The Battle of the Bill

Money can be a really tough topic for couples, but it can be an even more awkward and confusing issue on a date. We simply can't expect guys to pick up the tab all the time, girls. There are many men out there who do not ask girls out and rarely ever date simply because they can't afford it. Think about it—shit's expensive nowadays. Even a "cheap" dinner and a movie can run a guy seventy-five bucks before you even split dessert. And not all of the awesome, hot, sweet, respectful men out there are rich. That cutie who you thought you had a strong connection with but only invited you over for sex might have actually wanted to date you. He just let his LSE♥ about not being able to afford it get in the way of asking you out on a proper date.

Most of the time, in order to find a good, honest, fair, loving relationship, you need to let go of the idea that the man should always pay. Here is another reason: a lot of guys are confused as hell about the whole idea of feminism and are actually worried that they will offend you by paying. They're concerned that you'll think that you "owe" him something if he buys you dinner. And (be honest) some of you independent chicks feel this way, too. You feel uncomfortable letting him pay your way, especially on a first date when you hardly even know him. This makes you feel beholden to him or guilty if you secretly hate his guts and want to sneak out the bathroom window while he's paying said bill. We really can't blame men for being confused about this one.

So what's a girl to do when the check comes on a date? Well, like most things, it depends on the situation. First of all, who asked who out? If it was a mutual "let's go out" kind of thing, then we think you should offer to split it. If he grabs the check, say something like, "How much do I owe you?" If he refuses your money, fine. At least you offered. Or if you're out for drinks and he buys the first round, offer to buy the second. He may not let you, but we think this is a show of good faith and independence that you should definitely put forward. But if you took our advice and asked him out, then we think you should at least be prepared to pay for it, so choose a place that you can afford. Don't ask him out to a concert and then expect him to pay! If he throws down his AMEX before you can, that's fine. Thank him graciously and offer to take him out for an after-dinner drink. Remember, you asked him out, so it's only fair that you follow through.

However, if he officially asked you out on a proper date like a gentleman, and he picked the restaurant and maybe even picked you up, then you can pretty much assume that he's going to pick up the tab, too. He wouldn't take you to the Four Seasons if he couldn't afford to take you there. In this case, let him pay and make sure to thank him. It would still be nice if you want to offer to split it, but be warned that there's always a chance he'll take you up on it. A guy once took us to a nice-ass dinner, and when the bill came we decided to do the reach. We were shocked when he said (in a cocky voice), "Thanks. You probably make more money than I do, anyway." Well, we hope that doesn't happen to you, but in a way it was worth it, because that three hundred dollar dinner saved us a lot of time and energy that we might have otherwise wasted on that jerk.

Dating Dialogue

First dates can make us feel like we're back in sixth grade when we needed a written list of conversation topics in hand before we could call a guy. (We totally did that, didn't you?) What you say and how you say it are really the most important things on a first date. This is your only chance to let him know the real you while at the same time not revealing *too* much about you. You can look perfect, wear the cutest Betsey Johnson dress on the planet, and have really great smelling lip gloss, but if you say stupid things or don't say enough, your first date will probably be the last.

But don't worry. We have broken it down into some very official rules on what to talk about (and what not to talk about) on a first date. You've probably already heard that you should never talk about politics or religion with a new person, but there are other topics you should avoid, too. Reread this list before every first date and pretty soon the only "wrong" things coming out of your mouth will be some very sexy dirty talk.

Dating Dialogue Do's

Do Compliment

We are not saying that you should blow smoke up this guy's ass (literally or figuratively). However, it makes people feel comfortable and flattered if you say one nice thing about them, so start the night off on the right foot. Say, "I like your shirt," or "You have such nice blue eyes." It will make him smile and give him the confidence he needs to tell you how pretty your hair looks. Pick something honest (and we promise, you can find something to compliment about anybody) and tell him. And please don't worry that he'll think you want to go downtown on him if you say one nice thing. If he does, then he's a wanker and at least you know that now!

Do Remember Your Manners

We don't care how independent you are—if he holds the door for you, say "Thank you," and if he offers you something, say, "Yes, please," or "No, thanks." This may sound really elementary and condescending, but we've actually seen some of our friends totally forget their manners around guys. Also, remember that it's not polite to talk about anything too graphic on a first date. Don't tell him the details of your last stomach flu, and don't feel like you can burp and then blow it in his face. We're not saying to censor yourself, but that's just plain rude.

Do Talk About Yourself

We don't want you to brag, but we do give you full permission to make yourself sound cool, because you *are* cool! Sometimes we girls feel uncomfortable talking about ourselves because we're scared of coming off as vain or conceited, but that is nonsense. If you go on and on about how many beauty pageants you won as a child, that would be annoying, but tell him about your job, your dreams, your passions, and your accomplishments. Guys like women who have their shit together, so let him know how much you've got going for you. But don't talk about job stuff all night— let him know the real you, too. Tell him about your family, your hobbies, and your favorite books and movies. Don't wait for him to start flapping his jaws; initiate conversation by offering things about yourself and your dialogue will start to flow freely.

Do Ask Questions

Yes, we want you to tell him about yourself, but it's not all about you, honey. In order to act interested, you need to be inquisitive.

There is always a chance that this dude only wants to talk about himself and won't ask *you* any questions. In this case, he is definitely obnoxious as hell, but he is actually doing you a favor. First, you won't have to bother asking any questions, and second, you'll know for sure not to waste your time on a second date with him. We love people who save us time. Anyway, get out of your head, stop wondering if you have lipstick on your teeth, and take this chance to get to know him. Ask him about his job and his dog and his mom and his favorite food. Oh, and ask him when his birthday is so that you can run home and open up your giant astrology book to find out how good or bad of a cosmic match you two will be.

Do Tell Him What You Like

If you like this guy and you want to go out with him again, let him know how he can make you happy. Say things like, "I love surprises," or "I like sushi and my favorite sushi place is on Seventh Street." If he's smart (and we really hope he's smart), on your next date, he'll probably surprise you with dinner from Sushi on Seventh Street. Guys will actually appreciate this insight because it will make their jobs easier. Just don't take this too far and say things like, "I've always liked five-carat diamonds in a princess setting." He really doesn't need to know that right now.

Dating Dialogue Don'ts
Don't Complain

No matter how much the service sucks or how bad traffic was, do not spend your first date griping about petty shit. Laugh it off instead, because bitching and moaning about small things will scare the crap out of this poor guy. He will immediately picture you screaming at waiters for twenty years and then eventually doing the same thing to him. Plus, if you manage to keep a good attitude about annoyances, you'll end up having a better time, too. Don't let cold soup ruin your chance to find love. Save the drama for your mama and enjoy this first date experience, no matter how annoying it may be.

Don't Talk About Exes

Don't you dare say one word about your ex-boyfriend or your ex-husband or your ex-guy friend with benefits on a first date. You are on a date with a *new* guy. No one else in the world matters right now. Give this guy your undivided attention and play by the golden rule♥. Do you want to get all gussied up for a first date and then sit there and eat fondue while you hear details about how his ex-girlfriend was a gold digger who liked to diddle women? We didn't think so.

Don't Bring Up Your Kinks

If you are a confident, empowered Hot Chick with seven butt plugs and eight dildos at home, then good for you, but we really don't think this guy needs to hear about it on your first date. Sure, you want to make sure that you're sexually compatible, but why not determine if you're compatible as people first? If you let him get to know you as a human before giving him too many details about what gets you off, he'll end up respecting you way more in the long run. Plus, if this guy isn't quite as sexually adventurous as you are, then he will probably be scared shitless (even without the butt plug).

Don't Talk About Babies

If your timeline says that you have to be married and pregnant within a year, then you should be honest about what you want, but not *too* honest. So tell him that you are looking for something serious, and tell him that you are hoping to start a family at some point in the relatively near future, but do not treat him like a sperm donor. Of course, if he says that he doesn't want to get married and have babies for another ten years, then he's not for you, but it's also amazing how much a man's timeline can change once he falls in love. So give him at least a few dates to get to know you before you suggest a trip to the fertility specialist "just to check things out." If you don't, that might be the last time you see his sperm in this lifetime.

Don't Talk About Your LSE ♥

If you even dream of saying something along the lines of, "I'm not sexy," or "I used to be in good shape but now I'm fat" on a date, then we are going to hunt you down, come to your house, and punch you in the face. This guy is on a *date* with you, ladies. He wouldn't be there if he didn't find you attractive, so shut up. Don't tell him you're not sexy, or he might believe you! And don't tell him that you're fat, or he might start looking for fat! The last thing in the world you want to do is put a negative impression of yourself in this guy's head, so focus on the positive and let him do the same.

Second Date Decision

Second dates are pretty major. He might try to have sex with you (yikes). You might actually *have* sex with him (super yikes). And afterward you'll have to decide whether or not this guy is worthy of a third date, after which you'll pretty much officially be dating (holy crap). Well, relax Hot Chicks. If you listen to your gut, you should already have a pretty good idea about whether or not a second date is in the stars. However, there are times when it's not totally clear. Just remember that whatever decision you ultimately make, it was the right decision simply because you made it. If you still want help, here is a fun quiz that will make the decision to ditch him or date him clearer than daylight. Start on neutral ground with zero points and see where you end up.

Second Date Decision: The Quiz

Question 1:
At any point during the first date, did it feel like the world stopped and it was just the two of you in a little romantic bubble?

If yes—Add 15 points

Question 2:
Was there anything inherently creepy about him, like the sound of his voice or some of the questions he asked you? Or did he do something super weird like read you a children's book that he had stored in the glove compartment of his Honda?

If yes—Subtract 20 points

Question 3:
Did you ever find yourself staring at his lips hoping that he'd kiss you, or did you really like the way he smelled?

If yes—Add 10 points

Question 4:
Was it awkward? Were there at least two painfully awkward silences and were you constantly searching for something to say?

If yes—Subtract 5 points

Question 5:
Did he make you laugh in any way, whether it was with his sexy charm, an actual sense of humor, or goofy jokes?

If yes—Add 9 points

Question 6:
Were you abnormally drawn to your BlackBerry? Did everything he say make you wish you were at home watching a rerun of *Friends* that you've already seen more than seven times?

If yes—Subtract 5 points

Question 7:
Did you feel relaxed and at ease after the first few minutes of the date? Even if there weren't super fireworks, did he make you feel calm and safe and content?

If yes—Add 10 points

Question 8:

Did he have a wandering eye, send text messages under the table, or make you feel like he would have rather been scooping up dog shit than having coffee with you?

If yes—Subtract 5 points

Question 9:

Did you find out on the first date that you have more friends in common than you thought or discover that you have other random stuff in common, like you both drink black coffee and put way too much parmesan cheese on everything?

If yes—Add 10 points

Question 10:

Did he give you any wussy or backhanded compliments like, "I would tell you how pretty you are, but you probably hear that all the time," or did he insult you in any way, even if it was just rolling his eyes at something you said?

If yes—Subtract 10 points

Question 11:

Was it nice that you didn't have to think too hard about what to say? Were you able to chat about things in a way that felt natural?

If yes—Add 10 points

Question 12:

Did he make inappropriate sexual comments or touch you in any way that made you uncomfortable? Did he reach over the table and grab your nose and say, "Got your nose!" or did he try to feel you up while you were watching *Passion of the Christ*?

If yes—Subtract 12 points

Question 13:

Did time go by really quickly on your date? Did you suddenly look around and realize that you'd closed down the restaurant or glance at your watch and discover that you'd been chatting for four hours?

If yes—Add 15 points

Question 14:

Honestly, are you totally not attracted to this guy for no good reason whatsoever? Would you rather make out with your brother than grab his ass?

If yes—Subtract 10 points

Question 15:

Did your stomach flip over at least once at some point on your first date?

If yes—Add 15 points

Scoring:

Once you add up all of your points, if you are in the plus, that is if you have any points whatsoever, you should definitely go on a second date with this guy. This means that even if things weren't perfect and fireworks didn't go off and blow up the bar, he either made you laugh or made you comfortable and there was at least a shred of chemistry or compatibility. We think that these things totally warrant a second date! You have nothing to lose except maybe an hour or two of your time, and you'll have much more information about this dude after just one more date, so do it! This guy could be the dream man that you built, or your next long-ass relationship that breaks your hot little heart, or he could end up just being a big bad boy test from the universe♥. But you'll never know unless you give him a second chance. So, if this dude scored some points with you, go out with him again, pay attention to your intuition, and at least give him a shot to score some more.

We realize that this quiz is very forgiving, and we did that for a reason. So if you took the quiz and you had something like negative twenty-five points, please do not waste any more of your heyday♥ on this loser. Sorry, we don't mean to call people names; we're just saying that if he lost that many points when he was trying to make a good impression, then he's a loser. And sorry, Hot Chicks, we don't care how cute he is—you can't date a loser. He won't make you feel good, and if the first date went that poorly, it's not going to get any better. Don't give it another thought. Just store him in your bad-date memory bank and laugh about it with your girlfriends. Don't waste your time getting down on yourself about it or down on men. Just keep sending out all of your positive, good vibrations while you go prowling for your next date.

The Second Date

If you go on a second date with a guy, it means that he is cool enough for you to make time in your busy Hot Chick life to see him again and that he has enough of the qualities you are look-ing for to make you think that he poses relationship potential or at least prospective heyday♥ fun. But going on a second date also begs some important questions, like is he cool enough to get intimate with and dedicate more of your time to getting to know? More often than not, a second date is primarily a time for you to figure out whether or not a guy is worthy of a *third* date.

The most important thing for you to have on a second date is clarity. Before you even start curling your eyelashes, we want you to be super clear with yourself about what this second date is all about. Are you going out with him again because your first date was magical♥ and you've been having fantasy sequences♥ about him every night, are you only doing the second date thing because you have nothing better to do, or was he kind of lame on the first date but still squeaked by and passed the quiz, so you're giving him a shot to redeem himself? It doesn't matter why you are going; we just want you to know the reason. If you sit down to dinner with-out even knowing why the hell you're there, the whole process will just be more confusing for you.

Maybe your first date was so clouded by jitters, sweaty palms, and awkward moments that it was difficult to tell if you had any chem-istry. In this case, the second date gives you the opportunity to see him clearer and make a decision about this guy without nerves blocking your vision. Of course you might still be a little bit ner-vous on this date. If you're nervous in an excited, butterflies in the stomach way, that's a great thing. You can even take this opportunity to tell him, "Wow, I'm kind of nervous!" He'll probably think that's adorable. But if you're nervous in a worried way, then quit it. You've already spent an evening with this dude and you can do it again, so stop stressing. He likes you and he wanted to see you again, so have confidence!

It's quite possible that you were not totally acting like yourself on your first date, simply because you were focused on getting through it in one piece and keeping the conversation going. So this time, let down your guard and let him know who you really are. We still don't recommend talking about how many dudes you've slept with or any strange compulsions you may have, but you can avoid those topics and still be yourself. And while you're relaxed and acting like yourself, you really need to focus on your intuition. Pay attention and really listen to this guy. Notice your chemistry (or lack thereof), how you interact, and be on the lookout for red flags♥.

You need to pay attention so that at the end of the date you can make a confident decision about whether or not you want to keep seeing this guy. And if you've been doing your job, you will know. You may not be sure if he's gonna be the father of your babies or just a few more fun dates, but you will know if he has enough of the things on your list for you to keep spending time and energy on him.

Mixed Emotions

It is very frustrating that whether or not we continue dating someone is not 100 percent our decision. Sadly, our right to rendezvous is often taken away by some jerk who never calls again, sends a text three weeks after a magical♥ date, or turns into a creepy stalker right after dropping us off after the first date. All you can do is be clear about what you want and follow our advice to help you through all of these sticky scenarios that are preventing you from enjoying the dating game.

He Loves You, You Love Him Not

What's a Hot Chick to do when she goes on a date with a guy and realizes at the same time that she never wants to see him again and that he's head over heels for her? This will happen more and more now that you know you are a Hot Chick. Guys will fall in love with your fine vibes and you will be forced to "break up" with them before you're really even dating. It sucks when a guy fails the second date quiz worse than Bush failed as president, and then won't take a hint and just disappear like you wish he would. But listen: if he falls hard for you or is just so cocky that he can't believe someone doesn't want to date him, you must not feel bad. You do not have to apologize for not loving him back, nor do you have to give this guy a second (or third) chance just because he begged you. You owe him nothing; the only person you are obligated to is yourself!

So if you know that he wants more than you can give, set him straight as soon as possible. The longer you wait and avoid his calls and delete his e-mails, the longer he will keep calling. Please remember to play by the golden rule♥, ladies! You wouldn't want some guy leading you on, right? Then don't do it to him. Nip it in the bud as quickly as you can by using one of our foolproof dumping techniques. You can use these scripts in e-mails, voice mails, or person-to-person chats. (We don't recommend text messages or Post-its.)

Option #1: Be Semi-Honest

We don't think you should lie to this guy or send mixed messages, but once in a while it's okay to be less than completely truthful. You should really only do this if you think he would handle the truth badly, like if he is the super-sensitive type who cried on your first date or the opposite, a violent type, and you're worried about what he'll do if you just say, "I don't like you." If you choose this route, you still have to be clear. That means you don't have to lay your heart on the line, but you can't avoid the situation or build some elaborate web of lies either. Here are a few examples of what we mean:

> **"Hi Mike, thanks for asking me out again, but unfortunately the timing is really bad right now, so I'm going to have to say no."**

> **"Hi Mike, I'm sorry but I feel like we are looking for two different things right now, and so I really don't think that we should go out again."**

These work because they are nice and vague, but they also are not lies. Do not say that you just got back together with your exboyfriend or that you're too busy at work to continue dating. That is bullshit and if you throw that stuff around, you're only asking for more drama in your life.

Option #2: Be Honest

The next time he calls, answer the phone and say calmly, clearly, and nicely that you are not interested. Or e-mail him back and explain that you have no desire to continue dating him. Remember that you are a Hot Chick who is not afraid to say what she wants, so go ahead and get this over with before he falls further in love.

> **"Hi John, I hope you are well. Listen, it was very nice meeting you and thank you for the date the other night. I enjoyed our time, but I am not interested in anything further. You are great, but I'm just looking for something else. I'm sure you will meet someone else who is perfect for you."**

> **"Hi John, I'm trying this new thing where I'm gonna be completely honest, and I have to say that I'm not sure that we're on the same page or that I really see us going anywhere. Sorry to be so blunt, but I don't want to play any games or waste anybody's time either."**

The trick here is to remind him in the middle of dumping him that you're being honest. Even if he's a completely cocky dickhead, he can't argue with that!

Option #3: Be Uber-Honest

This is a little bit harder and should probably be saved for cases when you dislike this guy so much that you feel a burning need to tell him exactly why you never want to see him again, or he won't take no for an answer and you need to be a little bit harsh. Please don't be cruel, though, even in these circumstances. You never know when this guy will end up being your coworker or neighbor or friend's new flame, so you always want to end things on good terms (if possible).

> **"Hi Steve, I had an interesting time the other night, but I am afraid that I do not want to pursue this any further. I didn't feel**

a connection with you and I don't want to waste my time or yours. Please understand that I am not interested in friendship, either. I am focusing on dating right now and trying to find the person who is the perfect fit for me. Please don't mistake my honesty for harshness; I do wish you the best of luck."

"Hi Steve, I really appreciate your honesty in letting me know your feelings for me, but I am afraid I do not feel the same way. Please respect my wishes. I will not change my mind, and the more you pursue me, the further I am pushed away. There is someone great for you out there, but I am sure I am not the one."

You Love Him, He Loves You Not

It sucks so hard when you go on a date with someone who you want to see again, but he doesn't feel the same way. Oh, dear Hot Chicks, we know how you feel. It's terrible! You've been dying to meet a man who makes you feel magical♥, and the moment you do, you get rejected. Well, listen, ladies, he is not the one! We know you think he's perfect and you want to kiss him all over, but we also know for a fact that this man is not for you. He would not be rejecting you if he was the one for you.

If he doesn't call you after the first or second date, or if he just tells you right then and there that he doesn't want to see you again, please don't cry or push him or freak out. If he knows that he doesn't want you, there is nothing you can do to change his mind. (Nope, not even *that*. No matter how good you think you are, it will not make him want you to be his girlfriend if he didn't already want you to be his girlfriend.) Instead, follow these three easy steps to getting him out of your head so that you can start giving head to someone who deserves it.

Solace Step #1: Be Honest

Hot Chicks are honest and go for what they want, so if you like him but he doesn't call and ask you out again, then you should absolutely call him! He may be shy or LSE♥ and need to know for a fact that you are interested. Just pick up the phone and say something really simple like, "Hi Jonny, I had a great time the other night. Hope we can do it again!" If he doesn't return your call after that, then you're done. Don't sex-text him at 3 a.m. or drive past his house or anything else that might be construed as stalking. Just let him know that you dig him, and if he's too lame to get it together and ask you out, then at least you can sleep peacefully knowing that you tried.

Solace Step #2: Be Grateful

If this guy has flat-out rejected you, then as bad as it hurts, he is actually doing you a huge favor. He is saving you time and energy and even worse heartache. The longer you see someone and the deeper your feelings grow, the harder it hurts when you get dropped. Rewire your brain so that you totally understand that this guy is *not* for you. We're pretty sure you didn't write in your Build a Boyfriend list, "I want a man who doesn't call me back and who I have to convince to go on a second date with me." He is not the one, and the universe♥ is just testing you to see how good you are at treating yourself well.

Solace Step #3: Be Confident

Don't let some guy's rejection make you feel LSE♥! It's not your problem. You are hot enough, you are good enough, and if he doesn't call you back or act interested, that is *his* issue. Unless you did something creepy on your first date like talk about your imaginary babies or get too drunk and cry into your pasta, it's most likely his problem. He doesn't know what he wants, and most likely he's not committing because he is either not mature enough for a relationship, has BMS♥, is gay, is hung up on his ex, or is just simply lame. All of these are damn good reasons why you don't want him, anyway.

You Love Him, He Might Love You Back, But He's Confusing the Crap Out of You with Weird Mixed Signals

This one is quite possibly the worst, and it is so common that we could probably write a whole book about men and the completely strange mixed messages they sometimes send. Actually, someone did write that book (*He's Just Not That Into You*), and he made some very good points about why any sort of mixed signal whatsoever is exactly the same as a loud and clear "no." But this book isn't about what he's into; it's about you, and we are here to help you read his signals so that you can get what *you* want. We think this is far more important, anyway.

So what do you do when a fabulous first date ends with a kiss goodnight and a heartfelt "I'll call you tomorrow," and then you never hear from him or he sends you a text nine days later saying, "Sorry, been swamped, thinking of you, call you soon," but then he never calls? Well, Greg Behrendt would probably say that he's just not that into you, and you know what? He's probably right. We've dated so many guys like this, and we've found that it doesn't matter one iota why he's not into us or what his problem is or how he could possibly not understand how magical♥ our lives could be together. All that matters is that you handle these situations like the Hot Chick that you are, and that's what we're going to help you do.

Mixed Message Method #1: Tell the Truth

We know that a lot of our suggestions start with just plain, simple honesty, and that's for a very good reason. It really is the best policy, and if you hit a floundering, confounding relationship with a big dose of truth, things will instantly become clearer. Just tell him how you're feeling straight up, girls, but don't forget to remind him how busy, fabulous, and independent you are! Try this. Say to him,

> **"Hey, dude, I like you, and I'd love to see you again, but it seems like you're really unsure, so just let me know when you decide if you'd like to hang out again. I'm too busy to waste any more time on this back and forth thing."**

If you say this to him, we promise that he will show you his true colors right then and there. He'll either permanently fall off the face of the earth, or he'll be so turned on by your Hot Chick bluntness he'll be at your doorstep within the hour.

Mixed Message Method #2: Make Sure Your Brain Is Wired Correctly

We know from experience (unfortunately) that when a chap is all mysteriously unavailable and elusive, it can make you freaking crazy! You want to sit around and go over and over and over why he said this and why he did that and what he might be doing now and who or what he did before you. You absolutely cannot allow yourself to indulge in this behavior! Who cares what he said or did? This guy is being lame, and he is probably not the one for you. Quit wondering who this guy really is and why he's acting this way. You know exactly who he is. He is a noncommittal game player who is wasting your time. We hate repeating ourselves, but we want to remind you one more time that you did not write on your Build a Boyfriend, "I want a guy who makes me waste time trying to figure out his mixed messages." (However, if you did write this, then we're very sorry but we probably can't help you.)

Mixed Message Method #3: Keep Your Life Going

If you had a great date with a guy and now he's sort of disappeared or is being really flaky, it's hard not to sit around and waste time thinking about him. We know you don't want to make plans for this weekend because he might end up calling, and you don't want to go back to the Web site you met on in case he sees that you've been looking at other profiles since your fabulous date. But you are giving your Hot Chick power to some random guy who doesn't have the balls to love you properly, and that is not okay. So don't break plans to sit at home trying to analyze him or wait to make weekend plans until the last minute just in case he calls. Don't stare at your inbox waiting for an e-mail from him or stare at your phone waiting for it to ring and scroll through his old text messages while you wait. All this behavior does is suck your energy that should be spent sending out great vibes so that you can find someone who is worthy of all your sexy power.

Mixed Message Method #4: Don't Play Games

Oh, wow, this one is so darned tempting. If he's waited a week to call you, it can be so much fun to watch the phone ring with a satisfied smirk on your face and let it go to voice mail. We know that some of you Hot Chicks out there know this game really well. You wait in agony for him to make contact with you, and then when he does, you decide it's his turn to wait. You think you're making him nervous or jealous or intrigued, but the only person you're actually messing with is yourself.

If you play his game right back, you are giving him exactly what he wants. When he finally calls you and you let it go to voice mail, he's on the other end of the line saying to his buddy, "Thank God she didn't answer," or "Cool, I'll leave a message and then when she finally calls me back, I'll let her leave *me* a message, and then I can buy another week before I have to call her again." Pretty sucky, right? If you engage in this time-sucking behavior, you are making zero progress and are letting his childish actions stop you from acting like the honest Hot Chick that you are. Two wrongs don't make a right, so stop the games right now!

Mixed Message Method #5: Kick Him to the Curb

If you've tried being honest and he's still playing games, then it's time to get rid of him. You don't have time for this garbage. So just put him out of your head, move on with your life, and the next time he calls or e-mails or texts, say, "Thanks for getting in touch, but I'm looking for someone who will be honest with me and not play games, and I don't think that's you." Keep in mind that you should really only do this *after* saying the honest bit in method #1, or he might feel like this is coming out of nowhere. But more likely than not, he'll thank you for doing him this favor. Some guys are just freaking spineless and act vague just because they're scared to say they're not into you. In this case, don't be scared to say that *you're* just not that into *him*.

Dating Disasters

Dating can be downright awkward and messy, even if you're not having dinner or sex, and whether it's your first date or your tenth, you will most likely be faced with at least one disastrous dating situation. But have no fear! We are going to help you through each of the dating obstacles you might encounter, or at least the five most common situations that will make you want to cry. It can't all be rainbows and sunshine, but if you follow our advice you'll get through these catastrophes with your pretty hearts and bods unscathed.

Dating Disaster #1: Painfully Awkward Silences

We are not talking about run of the mill awkwardness anymore; we're talking about a level of awkward so high that it warrants this "disaster" label. It can be very unsettling when you're so desperate to make small talk that you start saying dumb shit like, "I really like these chairs; they're so comfortable," and all you get in response is some lame, weak, unattractive, half-assed agreement nod that makes you want to punch him in the face. Silence like this can be so bad that it makes you wish you could just wiggle your nose and disappear through a porthole, but we do have some advice for other ways to handle it.

Silence Solution #1: Ask Questions

In order to get through these silences without having an anxiety attack, you are going to need to strap on your imaginary balls and take control of this situation. Just use this as an acting exercise. Act interested and ask him a bunch of questions that he cannot answer in one word, such as, "So, tell me about your job. What exactly do you do in a typical workday?" or "Oh, you work in finance? Can you tell me the difference between a regular IRA and a Roth IRA?" A guy who's this quiet is probably either LSE♥ as hell or just an ass, so if you give him the opportunity to feel like an expert, he might start talking. It may be boring, but it's better than nothing, and you might end up learning something. (And if you do get the answer to that IRA question, can you please let us know? Thanks!)

Silence Solution #2: Just Say It

We don't want you to act like a bitch, but if he's making zero effort to get to know you, you have every right to stand up for yourself. It is not your job to just nod and smile. If his weirdly quiet mood is getting to the point of being rude, call him on it. Say, "I'm sorry, Jason, but your silence is making me uncomfortable. Is something wrong?" Or you can blame him less directly and say, "Wow, this is awkward, isn't it?" Sometimes just calling attention to a situation can make it better. He might realize how weird he's acting and get it together, and maybe in twenty years you'll be sharing a laugh over that awkward first date.

Silence Solution #3: Get Up Out of There

If he's not just quiet but silent in a really creepy way and you start having visions of his taxidermied mother in a rocking chair, you need to protect yourself and leave. This is why it's always a good idea to have your own car with you on a date, or another escape route, especially if it's a first date or a blind date and you have no idea how awkward it might be. Listen to your gut, and if you get a bad vibe from this guy, you do not need to sit through four courses of torture. Simply say, "Sorry, Lance, but I am going to call it a night," and leave. We don't want *you* to end up in that rocking chair, ladies.

Dating Disaster #2: When a Guy Talks About His Ex

We have noticed that many, many men (some of them good,

some of them bad) share the same lousy habit of bringing up ex-girlfriends when they're on a date with us. It really pisses us off. He is not with that chick anymore; he is with us. But it's like their minds have one track, from date to girlfriend to ex-girlfriend, and she ends up on his mind more than we would like. We hate this. We feel like it's disrespectful, uninteresting, and a huge red flag♥ about this dude who can't seem to focus on the present. But we've learned that there is a cause for everything, and there are actually many reasons that a guy might talk about his ex on a date. They're not all bad, either. We've broken down what he is likely to say and translated it into what it actually means and how you should react like the confident Hot Chick that you are.

Ex Example #1: No Comparison

We're not gonna lie to you. If a guy brings up his ex on a date, he is in fact comparing her to you. However, that can actually be a good thing. Hopefully, he learned something from that failed relationship, so don't be freaked out by questions like, "What are you like when you're drunk because my ex-girlfriend used to turn into a bobcat?" Granted, this may not make him the smoothest of all men, but we actually think that questions like this reveal several positive qualities. Not only is he being honest, but this question shows that he knows what he wants. He learned a valuable lesson from a failed relationship and added an important item to his list of nonnegotiables—*no bobcats.* You could take a lesson from this guy, ladies!

So your date doesn't want another slutty, drunk girlfriend. How do you react? Well, what you do *not* do is use this juicy bit of information about his ex to indulge in a bunch of destructive fantasy sequences♥ with her as the star. You don't imagine her as a sexy little bobcat tearing him to shreds and picture him bleeding from her wounds both physical and emotional. He is telling you something that he did *not* like about her, so let him know that you are different. Respond honestly and maybe take the opportunity to flirt a little. Say something like, "Oh, I get a little bit playful when I drink, but I'll probably just flirt with you a bit more than usual." We promise that she'll be out of his mind in no time.

Ex Example #2: Happy Memories (barf)

But what if his ex-girlfriend wasn't a horrible shrew? What if she was cute and sweet and he talks about her positively? Well, that's okay, too. We think that a guy who doesn't totally hate and resent his ex might actually have it together more than one who does. If he's had one positive relationship, then he's far more likely to have another good one—hopefully with you! So don't freak out if he seems to have genuinely liked her. Good for him. He's still buying *you* dinner, not her, so calm the heck down. Simply change the subject back to something the two of you have in common, and hopefully he'll get the gist that you don't want to spend your entire date dwelling on the past, no matter how much fun it was.

But of course, enough is enough, and you have to respect yourself, Hot Chicks. If he brings his ex up out of nowhere to say something complimentary more than once, we think you should call him on it. Why not say something like, "So what's the deal, are you still in love with her?" and see what kind of reaction you get? We love men, but they're not always that smart. He may truly not realize what he's doing, and you might get a really fascinating reaction out of him. Remember, if you're on a date with someone who you suspect might still be in love with his ex-girlfriend, you don't actually have that much to lose. You'll be able to tell everything by his answer to that question, so just go for it.

Ex Example #3: Love or Hate?

Some ex-girlfriend conversations, however, are giant red flags♥. One or two casual comments are forgivable, but be wary of a guy who talks about his ex incessantly. He may still be in love with her or he may be so full of rage and resentment toward her that he will be the worst boyfriend ever to you! Sometimes it's hard to tell which is which. Remember the teeny tiny line between love and hate. If he goes on and on and on about what a horrible bitch she was, he's not for you. He may just be way out of touch with his emotions and unable to admit that she's still holding tightly onto his balls. Basically, anything he says that seems hate-filled or angry is bad. You don't want some guy who's gonna freak out just because he dated a bitch named Mandy and your best friend Mandy is coming over for brunch. Passionate hate is still passion, ladies, and you don't want to date a man who feels passionately for any other woman but you.

Ex Example #4: Sex and the Ex

There are things that we never, ever, ever want to hear about on a date, and they include what his favorite position was with his last girlfriend and what she used to call his wiener. We're sorry, but we don't think there is any excuse for a guy to talk about banging another chick when he's on a date with you! We think that when a guy brings up sex with his ex on a date, you have to be clear. You have to tell him that it is inappropriate and that you don't want to hear about it. If he's still being a boner and doesn't understand, then you can flip it and say something like, "When we get back to my place, I'll show you my trophy from winning the tri-state blowjob contest." That should shut him up good.

Dating Disaster #3: When a Guy Is Rude to the Waiter

It can be downright humiliating when we're on a date with a guy who treats a waiter or bartender like a slave. We've seen guys say things like, "Hey, buddy, can we get some ice in this agua, por favor," to an Italian waiter or call the bartender "Bucko" for no good reason. This not only makes a really bad impression on us, but it also makes us look bad, which is just not fair. But we've come up with three tactics to get yourself out of this situation looking like the charming Hot Chick that you are.

Rude Response #1: Be Calm but Crafty

Don't start an argument when some dude is screaming at the busboy. More yelling will only make things worse. Just sit there and stare out the window, then once the busboy escapes, excuse yourself to the restroom and find him. Say something like, "I am so sorry about that. I don't even know that guy. This is a first date, and he is such a jerk." This will make the poor busboy feel better and hopefully also save him from losing his job.

Rude Response #2: Give Gratuity

If your date has been an overall ass all night long and treated the waiter with no respect, he'll probably show the same lack of respect in his tip, too. But you can make up for his shortcomings in this arena by slipping an extra twenty onto the table when your date has his back turned. You can also use a more extreme version of response #1 and go find the waiter and give him that twenty yourself. You can't erase your date's awful behavior, but you can improve the situation with your generosity.

Rude Response #3: Tell Him to Stop

We don't want you to start a fight, but you absolutely have our permission to call your date on his rudeness. You can say, "Adam, I used to wait tables and it's a really hard job. Why don't you give the poor guy a break?" Or if you think that's too subtle for this douche, say, "Adam, you are acting like a total dick to the waiter, and that is making a really bad impression on me." At the very least, he'll know in advance why you say no to another date with him.

Dating Disaster #4: When You Fuck Up ♥

As much as we hate to admit it, dating disasters are not always the guy's fault. Sometimes our nerves get the best of us and we end up putting less than our best face forward. This can make us feel so embarrassed and regretful the next day, but don't worry if this happens to you, Hot Chicks. We never said you had to be perfect. We have been there, and we have done each of these things more times than we'd like to put in print. Here is how to handle them as gracefully as humanly possible:

Lady Liability #1: You Got Too Drunk

This can happen very easily if you're too nervous to eat before the date and then gulp a couple of drinks down in hopes of liquid courage. Pretty soon, you're sticking your face into the peanut mix, rooting around in your cleavage for crumbs, and falling down on your way to the restroom. This is obviously not Hot Chick behavior, but we can help you earn it back. The first trick is to pay attention and realize as soon as it's happening. The moment you feel yourself crossing that tipsy line, stop drinking alcohol and start chugging water. Own up to it as quickly as possible but don't act overly apologetic. Say, "Sorry, this never happens to me, but I'm really feeling out of it. Can you take me home, and can we get a rain check?"

If it's too late and you already made a huge ass out of yourself and you actually have no recollection of how you even got home, then you need to just buck up and apologize. Call him up and say,

"Peter, I'm so sorry I got so drunk last night. I realize that I made a horrible impression, but that is really unlike me. I hope you'll give me a chance to redeem myself." He may not give you that opportunity, but at least he won't hate you for puking all over his car's new upholstery.

Lady Liability #2: You Cried

Hey, sometimes it happens, Hot Chicks. A dude can strike a nerve and make us really emotional for some reason, and we end up crying into the guacamole. In this case, excuse yourself, go pull yourself together, and when you get back to the table say, "I'm so sorry about that. I had a really hard day and everything just got to me." Remember that you're human and that showing your emotional side isn't always a bad thing. It's how you handle it that matters. Don't sit there blubbering at the table and say things like, "Oh, I'm such a mess. You're never gonna want to get involved with someone like me!" Just get it together, explain what's going on with you, and let him make that decision for himself.

Lady Liability #3: You Got Too Opinionated

Oh dear, did you end up telling him that he's a giant dick weed because he voted for a different *American Idol* contestant than you, or did you get into a screaming match about the election and end up throwing tortilla chips at his head? Well, you may have given him a strong Crazy Vibe, but all you can do is make the most of it. First of all, you should certainly apologize sincerely and humbly. Then show him that you're *not* crazy by having a sense of humor about the whole thing. Say, "Wow, we really got into it last night, huh? I wonder what all that crazy passion would translate into in bed." This will certainly score you another date so that you can determine whether or not he's gonna score.

Lady Liability #4: Your LSE♥ Acted Up

Sometimes, as confident as we are, our LSE♥ acts up at the most inopportune moments and we end up acting weird, disinterested, or insecure. This can really confuse guys. If you're oddly quiet on a date, he might think that you don't like him. Keep in mind that he is probably nervous, too, so you can go ahead and voice your feelings on your date. Say, "Dude, I'm nervous! Isn't that funny?" Or if the date's already over and you regret the way your LSE♥ reared its ugly head, call him up and say, "Sorry if I acted weird last night. I had a lot on my mind, but I would like to take you out and make it up to you." Being forthright and bold is really sexy, girls! Don't let this guy write you off so quickly; at least try to get yourself one more chance to let him see the real you.

Dating Disaster #5: When a Guy Is a Bad Kisser

Awkward kisses are very common, but they pale in comparison to *disastrous* kisses. A catastrophic kiss can be a very painful experience. An intimate moment has gone terribly wrong and you are left standing there feeling like an asshole with slobber all over your face. Gross! Unfortunately, we have had our share of bad kissing experiences, so we are going to break down how to deal with it like any good girlfriend would do.

Make-out Mishap #1: Smug Smoocher

Have you ever gone on a date with a guy who seems perfectly nice and humble and smart, and then when he goes to kiss you good night, he starts acting like some bad-ass, sexy-pants soap star? You know that guy who suddenly starts kissing you like he's in a movie with all these weird tongue things, probably thinking that he's being sexy as hell. It is such a letdown when this happens, but our solution to this problem is simple. Stop kissing him. Find a way out. Do anything to end the madness. There is no possible way that you will ever enjoy such an arrogant kisser. You will be in your head the whole time, and if you're not in the moment, you should get yourself *out* of the moment. Hot Chicks are honest chicks, and if this guy is honestly making you want to puke with his cocky, Casanova kisses, then say good night and get your ass home.

Make-out Mishap #2: Feeble Frencher
This is another disastrous buzz-kill. We're talking about the guy who gives you a weird, half-assed kiss, but holds your head in a grip you can't get out of. What's really weird about this guy is that sometimes he is super slobbery, sometimes he just sort of lightly licks your lips, which is incredibly irritating, and sometimes he does the opposite—he doesn't even open his mouth. But every time, he holds you tightly in a bizarre, uncomfortable lip-lock, and then doesn't really do anything. We have two ideas to help you through this mess. First, try to guide him into a normal kiss with your proper kissing abilities. Sometimes that actually works. It's possible that he was just starting off weak to feel you out, so let him know you're not a tiny little gecko and kiss him right. If that doesn't work, just stop kissing him. Pull away, smile, say, "Good night," and get out of there.

Make-out Mishap #3: Inappropriate Initiator
This happens when a date is going all right, but before you've even decided whether or not you like him, he jumps down your throat out of nowhere like a pit bull in heat. You could be on a blind date, in a church, watching *Schindler's List*, or in the middle of a fancy, upscale restaurant, but he doesn't care. This dude is so stoked to be on a date that he thinks he can lick your tonsils anywhere, anytime, in any way. This is so uncomfortable. You don't want to hurt his feelings, but you also feel kind of like a slutty

fourteen-year-old playing kissy-face like this. Just pull away and try to bring his attention to something else. If he keeps trying to lock lips with you, then you're gonna need to be a bit bolder. Stand up for yourself and say, "I'm not a prude and I'd love to kiss you, but this doesn't seem to be the appropriate time." If that doesn't work either, you know what to do: get your hot ass home in no time.

Third Date Thoughts

Third dates are major. If you go on three dates with someone, he is playing an actual role in your life and you will remember him for a long time. There is always a chance that things could go terribly wrong after a third date, but if your vibes are cool and you've been paying attention, it should be pretty clear by now that this guy is going to stick around for a while.

You should not see someone three times if you don't like him that much or if you know that he is totally wrong for you. If you go against your intuition, we promise it will never work. We all know some girls who will keep dating a guy who she's been complaining about since the *first* date. And the inevitable always happens— she ends up crying and arguing with him every other day and they end up breaking up a month later. Don't be that girl. Take a moment right now to step back and decide if you really like this guy enough to keep dating him. It's very important that you are not just going on a third date for shits and giggles—unless you're into that sort of thing.

However, there are some exceptions, depending on your intentions. If you're the girl who is dating just to date and you are unsure about going on a third, we say go for it! Have another fun night out and (if you want) enjoy some fun, messy sex. Celebrate your heyday♥ by dating this guy who is at least semi-interesting. However, if you aren't super into this guy and you're letting your time with him distract you from meeting other guys, then you should move on without a third date. Don't let one guy who you *kind of* like prevent you from sampling others. Also, if you've already met other guys you like more than this one, kick him to the curb! You don't need to waste this guy's time either, which you are doing if there are other boys twitterpating♥ you more than he is.

If you are looking for a boyfriend, our advice is a little different. We think that you should only go on this third date if this guy has the majority of qualities on your Build a Boyfriend list and hasn't raised any major red flags♥. Remember, you don't just want any boyfriend: you want a good one. Go back and look at your list and really think about it. If you're still unclear, then it's possible that you'll need to go on a third date in order to make a final decision about this guy. That's fine. But if you're looking for a relationship and you keep dating someone who you're not crazy about, it'll be like trying to satisfy a Mexican food craving with Taco Bell. The fake stuff may taste good for a bit, but you deserve something more authentic.

Finally, if you're looking for a husband, it's even more important that you give this third date some serious thought. If you know that this guy isn't the one, or you know that you don't really have chemistry, or you know that he isn't looking for a wife, then do not waste your time and energy on a third date. If you know he isn't the one but you still want to get laid or just have someone to see a movie with, we completely understand, but we still don't think you should. If your intention is to find Mr. Right and you spend too much time on Mr. Wrong, you are missing opportunities to find a perfect catch.

Chapter 5

Get Some Loving

NOW THAT YOU'RE GOING ON DATES AND FULLY ENJOY-
ING YOUR HEYDAY♥, IT'S TIME TO TALK ABOUT SEX,
BABY. We're not sexperts; we're just two girlfriends who have
struggled with our own insecurities and confusion in the bedroom,
and we've learned a thing or two through both disappointments
and pleasures (plus a ton of girl talk, of course). We're not going
to get into the technical stuff, but we're here to help you figure out
when to do it, why to do it, and how to always do it feeling like an
empowered, sexy Hot Chick.

Sex is messy, and it can be so in ways both good and bad. Most
women, no matter how experienced, share the exact same insecurities and questions when it comes to getting intimate. We all
have the same body issues, fears of abandonment, need for attention, jealousy, and insecurities when it comes to "performance."
And we definitely all get emotional when it comes to sex.

When you're dating, the decisions you make about sex will probably have an impact on your relationships with men and your self-esteem for the rest of your life. And we don't want confusion around these decisions to get in your way of finding true love. This chapter will steer you through every sexual decision and obstacle you will face on the dating scene, and pretty soon you'll be having more fun in the bedroom than you ever imagined. Buckle up, girls; we hope it's going to be a bumpy ride.

Virgin Validation

We want to spend a minute talking to all you Hot Chicks who are still holding onto your beautiful virginity. Whether you're saving yourself for marriage or just your first true love, we think that is fantastic. Sex is very powerful, and who you sleep with has an impact on many aspects of your life. There is no need to rush it. We are all ready to have sex at a different time, and you will definitely know when you are ready. Listen to your body and your heart, not to anyone else who is pressuring you to have sex. Your first sexual experiences will color your sexual experiences for the rest of your life. If you wait until you find the right person and situation, this can be a good thing, but if you do it too soon or for the wrong reasons, it will definitely hurt you in the long run.

If you are a virgin Hot Chick, we are so proud of you! Please hold onto it until the timing is right, and don't let anyone else tell you when the time is right for you. Do not let some horny boy pressure you into doing things you are not comfortable with. If the things he's trying to force you into don't sound appealing, then you're not ready, and that is totally normal. For others of you, the things he's talking about doing might intrigue you, but that still doesn't mean you should take the plunge. Really think about whether or not you are ready to engage in these powerful, special, intimate acts with this person. Just because something sounds intriguing, that doesn't mean you shouldn't wait until you find the right person to do it with.

In the meantime, take this time to educate yourself. Learn about sex and what sounds like fun to you, and experiment with yourself until you find the right guy. It's perfectly healthy to be curious and learn all about it—that doesn't mean you have to do it right away. And while you are a lovely virgin, remember to always act like a Hot Chick and never play small♥. You have absolutely nothing to apologize for, so be proud of your status! You can still have an amazing heyday♥ without having sex. Enjoy the power of your virginity and take pleasure in the process of waiting until you just can't wait any longer.

(Of course, if you are a virgin for unhealthy reasons, like you have some deeply rooted fears or a history of abuse, please take care of yourself and get help. Work through your issues so that you can come out on the other side ready and willing to love.)

Vexing Virgins

Now we need to talk to you girls who call yourself virgins but are actually acting slutty and giving those beautiful, real virgins a bad name. We are talking to you if you call yourself a "born again virgin" just because you haven't gotten laid in a month or you say you're a virgin but give blow jobs to your school's entire football team and let anyone with a tongue go downtown on you. Actual virginity is a sacred, beautiful thing, and if this behavior above describes you, then you are not only *not* a virgin, but you're also not a Hot Chick. Instead, you are acting like an attention-starved LSE♥ girl with acutely fucked up♥ vibes.

If this is you, quit batting your eyelashes about how wonderful you are for not having intercourse, because you're no better than anyone else. Stop reclaiming your virginity during every dry spell and stop bragging to boys about your virginity and letting them lick your ass two seconds later. Sorry to be crude, but you are taking something away from all the Hot Chicks out there who are genuine about their sexuality. You're acting like a girl who boasts about being a vegetarian but eats Big Macs when she's hungover.

Please note, we are not saying that you can't enjoy sexual relations if you are a virgin! If you like to get some kisses and experiment but you're being choosy about who you go all the way with, we're not referring to you. That all sounds great. Let us be clear: we are talking about girls who say they are virgins *in order to get sexual attention from men*. If you brag about your virginity because you're whoring around with vanity, you're just like a governor who cracks down on prostitution and then gets caught in bed with an $800,000 hooker. If you want to sleep around or make out with everyone you know, that's fine. We won't judge you. But don't play the virgin card, or we'll have to call bullshit on you. Be honest and respect yourself, and everyone else will have an easier time respecting you, too.

Bedroom Bylaws

Alrighty, now it's time to move on to those of you who are actually having sex. Well, unfortunately, making love is rarely as glamorous as the movies make it seem. It is actually very unusual for sex to be effortlessly perfect and harmonious, but we want to steer you clear of anything awkward or uncomfortable so that you can end up basking in bedroom bliss. Here are some very important Hot Chick rules for making your lovemaking magic♥.

Bedroom Bylaw #1: Take Control

We don't mean that you have to throw your guy against the wall and initiate *everything*, unless you're into that, but we do want to remind you not to lie there like a rag doll. It takes two to tango, girls, and it's not all up to the man to make sex good. You have to perform, too. Take a little bit of control and help guide things in the right direction. You have the power to make this experience memorable and delightful for both of you.

Bedroom Bylaw #2: Be Genuine

You are a Hot Chick, and you do not need to do anything that's out of your comfort zone in order to impress this guy. Do not act like some crazy nympho-slut-goddess because you think it will make him like you more. Of course you should be open to new things and willing to try whatever he likes, too, but always be true to yourself. Your body is *your* body, and if you let someone have you in a way that makes you queasy, you will end up resenting him and losing respect for yourself.

Bedroom Bylaw #3: Talk

Whether you talk dirty or not is none of our business, but you should always keep communication with your guy flowing. Some women get scared silent during sex, which can make men feel really LSE♥ in the bedroom. (And that always ends badly.) Don't let your muteness ruin this experience for both of you. You shouldn't be afraid to say what you like, ask what he likes, or at least make some noises in agreement.

Bedroom Bylaw #4: Be Safe

You have absolutely no excuse for getting so wrapped up in the moment that you forget about birth control and get yourself knocked up. Take responsibility for your body so that you don't end up with an accidental baby or a lifelong disease. Seriously, there is so much nasty stuff out there and so many guys don't even realize that they have it. Make him wrap his package up, and if he balks for any reason whatsoever, find someone who will be delighted to wear a condom if it means the chance to have sex with a girl who's as hot as you.

Bedroom Bylaw #5: Be Honest

Sex is the most intimate act that two people can engage in, so if you are comfortable enough to jump into bed with him, you better be comfortable enough to be honest with him! Do you have an STD? Are you not on the pill? Did you forget to put your sponge in? Whatever it is, if you feel like you should probably tell him, then you should definitely tell him. You don't want to sleep with him and find out three days later that he has some deep, dark secret. And you don't want to make out with him tonight and discover that you have mono tomorrow. Give him the respect he deserves: act like a Hot Chick, and be honest!

Bedroom Bylaw #6: Don't Be LSE♥

You are gorgeous and sexy and powerful, and you have a beautiful womanly body and this dude is *lucky* to have an opportunity to see you in your birthday suit. Don't you dare get all LSE♥ and self-conscious about your body! If you are playing small♥ and telling him not to look at you, or you're only doing it in a pitch-black room under the sheets, we want to help you. You are hot and you have nothing to apologize for! He wants to have sex with you, and that means that he is attracted to you, so let it all go and let yourself enjoy the moment. We promise it'll be a lot more fun as soon as you stop sucking it in and start sucking on something else.

Bedroom Bylaw #7: Don't Compare

The bedroom is the single most inappropriate place to talk about your past lovers. Do not make reference to the stack of Magnum Condoms on your nightstand; do not tell him how you discovered your favorite position; and do not utter any sentence that begins with, "I really liked it when my ex-boyfriend . . ."

Bedroom Bylaw #8: Get Out of Your Head

It's time to turn off that inner monologue and focus on this guy and what your bodies are doing. Stop thinking about that memo you have to write for work, what you're going to have for breakfast tomorrow, or what the neighbors are thinking. And don't get all up in your head worrying about what *he's* thinking. We promise that you won't be able to read his mind no matter how hard you try, so save yourself the trouble. If your mind wanders during sex, he will probably notice and get all LSE♥, and everything will go to shit. Stop the madness before it starts by turning off your brain and turning on your body.

Bedroom Bylaw #9: Don't Say Weird Shit

Sometimes when we get lost in intimate moments, we end up blurting out things that are super strange. Do not giggle while he's banging you and say, "Oh, sorry, I was just thinking about a scene from *Anchorman*." Do you think he really wants to know that you are thinking about Will Ferrell while he's screwing you? We're not saying that you should censor yourself, but some things translate really poorly in the bedroom, so think twice before saying something that will make him lose sleep that night.

Bedroom Bylaw #10: Tell Him What You Like

This goes hand-in-hand with being honest and taking initiative. Don't be critical or cruel, but feel free to let him know which of his moves you prefer and how he can satisfy you even more. If he's sucking on any part of your body like a Dyson and it's seriously turning you off, say something like, "It's really hot when you kiss me gently right there." If he's sticking his tongue in your ear and it's making you want to puke, say, "I'm sorry, my ears are really ticklish, but I love it when you lick me right there . . ." Another trick is to do to *him* the things you wish he would do to you. If you're dying for him to get a little rough, then bite his neck and scratch his back. If you two are compatible, he'll be reciprocating in no time.

Sex and Dating: The Game

It's time to help you through some major sexual decisions, like *when* you should or shouldn't have sex and *why* you should or shouldn't have sex. Admit it: have you always been completely clear and correct in all of your choices about sex? Many of you are probably giving it up too soon or holding out too long, and are confusing the universe♥ by making the wrong decisions. But whether you are Pretty & Prowling, Beckoning for a Boyfriend, or Waiting to Wed, we have the answers to some of your burning sex questions. (Oh, but we really hope there's no burning!) We also have a bunch of exceptions (or *sex*ceptions), because no good girlfriend would let you sleep with someone (or not sleep with someone) without giving you at least one reason why you did the right thing.

Should You Have Sex on the First Date?
Answer:
No!

Reason:
We don't care how heydayish♥ you are, there is no good reason for you to let this guy have it all on night one. We want you to protect yourself, and we don't just mean by using a condom. (However, we definitely want you to do that, too.) We want you to protect your heart and your hot little head, as well. Having sex with a guy too soon, before you really know if you even like him, can mess with your judgment and make you feel incredibly LSE♥.

Some of you may be strong enough to handle this, but we know that it will make most of your emotions go haywire, and you'll end up attaching too much emotion to a guy you barely even know. What if you think you really like him, but then he never calls you again? How will you feel then? What if the sex is terrible and you realize you don't even like him, but then he won't stop calling? Or what if the sex is so terrible only because you aren't comfortable around each other yet, but it could have been magical♥ after just two more dates? Just wait a minute and get to know him a little tiny bit before you let him see you naked. Jumping into bed with him too soon will get you nowhere but a strange place with weird sheets and no clue where the bathroom is.

Sexceptions:

If you are dating just to date and you know yourself well enough to know that sleeping with this guy is a 100 percent healthy decision for you, then go for it! Don't let *us* stop you from gettin' some. If you're sure that letting this guy have all your goodies will not mess with your head and you have completely accepted the fact that you may never see or hear from him again, you have our full permission to move forward. In this case, you are telling the universe♥ that you are a Pretty Prowler who just wants to keep things casual. Enjoy it and always remember to be safe.

You can also have sex on the first date if you are a Pretty Prowler and you want to experience a potential one-night stand. Just follow all of our one-night stand rules on page 149 and be prepared for some confusion about whether this was, in fact, a one-night stand, or if it was a first date that ended in sex. As long as your head is okay with either one, then go ahead with the head. But again, be safe. It would really suck if you got yourself something nasty or got knocked up.

If you are looking for a relationship or a husband, then we're very sorry, but there are no sexceptions for you. Sleeping with someone on date numero uno will only confuse the universe♥ about your intentions, so hold out for a while and see if there's any future between you before hitting the sheets.

Should You Have Sex on a Second Date?
Answer:
Probably not

Reason:
It's still too soon. It really is. It's great that you liked him enough to go out with him twice. That means there is actual potential here! But you still don't know if he's going to get totally weird after you sleep with him, or if you're going to get totally weird after you sleep with him, or if it's just going to be really weird to sleep with him. Enjoy an innocent make-out session and leave yourselves something to look forward to. After all, anticipation is half the fun, right?

Sexceptions:
If you are dating just to date and you thought about having sex with him on the first date but wanted to give yourself one more chance to make sure, then good for you. If you have just as much fun on the second date, go ahead and jump into bed. Also for you Pretty Prowlers, all of the same rules apply here as for first date sex. If you are completely comfortable or looking for a one-night stand, be our guests.

And this time, we will make a sexception for you other gals, too. If you are Beckoning for a Boyfriend or Waiting to Wed and you have a giant, magical♥, magnetic physical attraction to this guy, you can have sex on the second date. You may only do this if you two had so much chemistry on both dates, so many laughs, and so much flirty talk that you really, truly can't help yourself. If you get talked into it or you force it for the wrong reasons, we promise you will not be a happy camper. Remember that there are still many risks here, because you don't know enough about this guy to be sure if he is good enough for you or if he wants the same things as you. If you're so compatible that doing it on the second date feels totally natural, just understand the potential consequences, know that he may end up not being "the one," and enjoy the experience.

Should You Have Sex on a Third Date?
Answer:
Probably

Reason:
If you are dating just to date and by the third date you haven't had sex yet—either because you aren't attracted enough to him or he's being wishy-washy about making a move—then he's probably not worth any more of your time. You don't want to date someone you don't have chemistry with, and you Pretty Prowlers don't need to sit around waiting for chemistry to build as you get to know each other on a deeper level. We're not saying that dating is all about sex, but we also don't want you to settle for someone who's unworthy of your hotness, especially at this point in your life.

If you're looking for a husband or a boyfriend, pretty much the same thing goes for you. If you've made it successfully through three dates and you are attracted to this guy, there's no reason to hold off any longer. Now is a good time to shit or get off the pot, fish or cut bait, or whatever cliché works for you. Test out the goods before you get even more attached, just in case a major deal-breaker rears its ugly head just when you're about to give some.

Sexceptions:

If you are a virgin or very young—let's say under twenty-three—and are dating just to date or looking for a boyfriend, it's okay not to have sex with someone after only three dates. You girls have plenty of time to date around, so feel free to do so without adding too many notches to your headboards. Don't apologize: just be clear with the guys you date about what you're looking for and only have sex with them when you are totally ready.

Another sexception is if you are looking for a serious relationship or a husband and you think this guy might be the one. In this case, it might be smart to hold off for just a little while longer. These first few sex-free dates are your only chance to get to know each other without the sex clouding your judgment. Plus, if you really think this guy has serious potential, then the sex you ultimately have with him will be better the longer you wait. You'll be more comfortable around each other, and it will actually mean something if you allow your feelings for each other to grow beforehand.

Should You Have Sex on a Fourth Date?
Answer:
Yes!

Reason:
At this point, if you want to have sex with him, you should do it! But if you've gone on four dates with someone and you still aren't feeling it, you probably never will. Four dates is a lot of time and energy spent on one person, so if you're not dying to jump in the

sack or get a look at his, he probably doesn't warrant any more of your attention. This doesn't mean that there's anything wrong with him (or you). You two probably just aren't meant to be and don't have a lot of chemistry. Don't waste your time wondering why or trying to change the situation: just turn your attention to finding someone else who won't raise so many questions.

Sexceptions:

The only real sexception here is if you're a virgin. If you are and you're holding out for marriage or even engagement, then go ahead and go on hundreds of dates without sex. Of course, be clear with the guy about your status and if he's not cool with it, then dump him immediately and find someone else who is.

How to Tell If a Man Is Good in Bed in Three Easy Steps

While many of you have been surreptitiously measuring your date's hands, feet, and ears for signs that he might be endowed with other prized qualities, we have discovered three far more reliable ways to find out if a man will be able to please you in bed before you engage in any remotely sexual activities. Follow these quick steps while you're on your first and second dates, and we'll save you from regrets, awkward moments, and even some fairly significant cash on condoms.

Step #1: Watch Him Eat

In our studies, we have uncovered a direct correlation between a man's hunger for food and his appetites in the bedroom. That's why we try to always eat a meal (or if we're feeling particularly heydayish♥, at least a late-night snack) with a man before bringing him home. We need to take a look at how he eats. Our findings show that men who are picky, count their calories, and limit their consumption are equally cautious and controlled in the bedroom—and if there's one thing we don't appreciate in bed, it is prudence. Our friend once dated a man who was very fussy about his food, and it did in fact end up mirroring how he treated her. He insisted on always hanging up his pants before getting into bed, even if the pants came off in the heat of passion. We don't think that's very hot, and so we've made it a rule not to date men who eat frozen yogurt as a meal or ever get full from eating a salad.

Conversely, a man who attacks his food like a starving animal is likely to do the same thing to you—and we likey. As a result, when our man orders chicken-fried steak and a milkshake for breakfast, stresses out that his giant sandwich might in fact be too small, or drinks a glass of whiskey when he mops the floor, we get a little bit turned on. We'd rather have a man with a few extra pounds to grab onto than one who turns out to be overly selective about what he puts in his mouth.

Step #2: Watch Him Fix Something (Anything)

We're not saying that all men have to be super handy, although that would surely be fine with us. It can be as simple as screwing in a lightbulb, but you absolutely must watch a man repair something in order to determine whether or not he will be able to get the job done in bed. It's all about precision, ladies, and a man who can make a bunch of distinct parts magically fit together or cross a million different wires in order to create a spark is way more likely to produce similar results with you. Make sure to pay close attention to how he reacts to his own efforts, too. If he gets frustrated and gives up easily, it's for sure a bad sign. But if he keeps plugging away, determined to get it right even if only to prove his manliness, you can skip the snack and go straight home—you've got yourself a winner.

Step #3: Watch Him Operate Heavy Machinery

In order to find out what kind of thong we're wearing, our man needs to know how to steer. It can be a car or a rowboat or a big giant tractor (that's hot), but a man who fumbles around with the gears or drops an oar or can't parallel park with the radio on probably won't be able to throw you around like you want without bashing your head into the wall. On the other hand, a man who rides that thing like it's a natural extension of his own body is definitely a keeper. Just picture yourself as being whatever object he's maneuvering, and if it looks like fun to you, then you're probably in good hands—or about to be.

One Night Only

Right after we declared it our heyday♥, we decided to celebrate by going to see a psychic, and that psychic told us something very profound. He said, "You should start having one-night stands." Well, he wasn't a very good psychic, but he was great at opening our mind. That one comment left us giggling and excited to jump into the dating sea with a new attitude and a more carefree confidence. We already knew what was on our list and what our intentions were, but this advice helped us let go of trying to find someone who was perfect and start seeing this whole dating process as fun.

The truth is we never ended up taking his advice, because we didn't have to. Instead, what happened was that by merely thinking that we might have a one-night stand, we became more open to going on dates with different kinds of guys—guys we might have previously written off. And ultimately, just having the mind-set of, "Well, if all else fails, maybe I'll just sleep with him," helped us find true love. And so, Hot Chicks, we want to give the same advice to you. If you are a sexually active, adventurous woman, open your mind to the possibility of a one-night stand. It can be a fun, unique heyday♥ experience, and just opening yourself up to it may leave you open to getting so much more.

Of course, one-night stands can have repercussions. They can be sticky and tricky and you have to be very careful about where, why, how, and with whom you engage in these encounters. So if you are going to partake in a one-time event, follow these rules to a positive, exciting experience.

One-Night Stand Rule #1: Do It for the Right Reasons

What are your intentions? What vibe are you sending? Are you LSE♥? If you are doing this to get attention from him, then you shouldn't be doing this. Only have a one-night stand if it's something you want to experience just for you. If you do it for any other reason, you will end up feeling like crap.

One-Night Stand Rule #2: No Total Strangers

Do not have a one-night stand with someone you met at a bar that night or on a first online date. Remember that Ted Bundy was kind of hot and charismatic, and his one-night stands ended up with more than a broken heart. We don't mean to scare you, but check with your intuition and check this guy out before you jump in the sack with him.

One-Night Stand Rule #3: No Coworkers

Having a one-night stand with someone you will have to face every day until you get a new job is just not smart, so don't do it, ladies.

One-Night Stand Rule #4: Protect Yourself

We really hope that we don't have to tell you to use condoms again. But just in case, here we go again—use condoms!

One-Night Stand Rule #5: Protect Him

Be honest with this dude. He may really like you. He may want you to be his girlfriend. Protect his feelings by being honest with him about what this night is about.

One-Night Stand Rule #6: Your Place, Not His

We think it is always preferable to stay on your own territory in these situations. You may get a few raised eyebrows from your roommates, but at least at your place you have clean sheets, clean towels, and clean underwear. These will all be comforting in the morning.

One-Night Stand Rule #7: No Crushes

Do not have a one-night stand with some guy who you've been harboring a secret crush on for six months! You will feel so sad and defeated when he leaves in the morning—or if he takes off before dawn. If you're looking forward to getting pancakes with him in the morning, he is not the right one-night stand for you.

One-Night Stand Rule #8: No Exes

Randomly having sex with your ex-boyfriend does not count as a one-night stand. It only counts as a poor decision.

One-Night Stand Rule #9: No Regrets

Before having a one-night stand, ask yourself these questions: Will I regret this if I never hear from him again? Am I going to feel like a dirty slut in the morning, or will I feel exhilarated? Would I enjoy sex with this guy more if I got to know him a little bit better? We are trying to help you avoid regret, ladies, because regret is a horrible, nasty emotion. Know yourself and do what's right for you, and you won't have to waste your time feeling ashamed.

One-Night Stand Rule #10: No Drunk Decisions

If it is the end of a long night of drinking and you are wasted, do not take some guy home with you. If you do this, you will probably end up breaking every single one of the above rules and feeling very sorry in the morning.

How to Tell If You Have Chemistry (Without Having Sex)

When you're dating, it can be easy to get confused about whether or not you're even attracted to a particular guy. You like him, you have fun together, maybe you even share some common interests and goals and all that other boring stuff, and he may have some of the things on your list, but are you really drawn to him? Sometimes we single gals want to be into a guy so badly—because he's nice and smart and would actually get along with our father—that we get all mixed up about whether he just looks good on paper or if we really do want to rip his clothes off. But even when our brains are overwhelmed or confused, our subconscious minds always know exactly what we really crave, and we're here to help you figure out your subliminal desires.

Chemistry Cue #1: Listen to Your Words
This is very important, ladies. When you first meet a guy and are in the initial stages of dating, pay attention to what you say to your girlfriends when he's not around. If you hear yourself saying things like, "I don't know, the thought of having sex with him seems like it could be kind of . . . awkward," then we have to go ahead and tell you that you probably don't have chemistry with this guy—or at least not the kind that will blow your skirt up, and that's the kind of chemistry that you Hot Chicks deserve! It's easy to find a guy who you'll love to talk on the phone or share a sundae with, but that doesn't necessarily make him your perfect lover. You want a man who wants to eat that sundae off of your hot body, right?

That's chemistry! Never underestimate the power of your words, ladies! If you keep saying that you're not sure it's there, then we're here to tell you it's not there.

Chemistry Cue #2: Get a Good Whiff

It's kind of a proven fact that we can't have chemistry with a guy who we think smells weird. Now, we're not talking about BO here—that is obviously not hot. We're talking about a guy's natural manly scent. Go ahead and give your guy a squeeze, nuzzle your nose in the nape of his neck, and just breathe. When you have crazy chemistry with a guy, you will think his pheromones smell like fresh-baked cookies, or maybe cinnamon. You won't be able to get enough of the intoxicating scent.

When you have magical♥ chemistry with someone, you may find that you even love the smell of his dirty T-shirts or think that his sweaty socks smell like popcorn. It's all about pheromones, and when you're truly, deeply attracted to someone, his stink can be as comforting as a cherry pie in the oven or the smell of your favorite grandfather's pipe. A friend of ours once told us that she finds it impossible to have an orgasm unless she sticks her nose directly into her guy's armpit during sex and breathes in his sweaty scent. Yes, we think that's kind of strange, but honestly, we've heard of way more peculiar ways of climaxing, and it's only natural for your dude's aroma to turn you on. You don't need to have sex with a guy to see if you have chemistry. Just give him a tight hug, get a good whiff, and see how you feel.

Chemistry Cue #3: Picture Your Babies

Now let us be *very* clear—we don't mean this in a psycho, crazy girl way! It is definitely not hot to get all moony and swoony after date number one and start having fantasy sequences♥ about what your wedding dress, children, and retirement home will all look like. That's not what we're talking about here. This is a way more constructive use of your time. Have you ever thought to yourself, if New York and San Francisco had a baby it would be Sydney, Australia? Well, same concept here—your imaginary baby is gonna have all of the qualities that you and this guy bring out in each other.

If you two are always laughing, then you might picture your baby popping out of your womb cracking jokes with a microphone in hand. Or if there is a lot of drama between you, your fake baby might be the tortured type who sets his college dorm room on fire in a fit of rage. Or maybe he's a brilliant actor who'll be born delivering eloquent soliloquies. Of course, if you guys are super cute together, you'll be amazed at how hot your make-believe baby is! If it's a boy and he's gay, that might mean that you suspect his father won't be so hot in bed. If your girl is a stripper, deep down you probably think this guy is trash. You get the idea—if you like your baby, then the dude is probably worth considering. But if the thought of your imaginary baby makes you want to run out and get your tubes tied, we're pretty sure you and the non-father aren't meant for each other.

Chapter 6

About the Boys

WE COULDN'T WRITE A BOOK ABOUT LOVE WITHOUT AT LEAST ONE CHAPTER ABOUT WHO IT IS WE'RE TRYING TO LOVE. This chapter is all about analyzing the men in your life so that you can make a clear decision about whether or not he can give you the love you deserve.

Men and women are wired differently and there is nothing we can do about that, but men are people, too. And just like people (and apples), there are good ones and there are bad ones. There are tons of super-cool guys out there who are ready and waiting to meet, date, and fall in love with an awesome Hot Chick like you, and there are also a bunch of dickheads out there who are immature, clueless about what they want, and will just keep playing you like Guitar Hero.

Well, we can't change your guy (and we hope you know that you probably can't change him either), but we can help you determine what kind of guy you're dating and give you advice on how to deal with him as he is. And we can certainly teach you what kinds of guys to never let within thirty feet of your hot body. Some of this may seem a little harsh, but we don't want you to settle for anything less than a wonderful man who will treat you wonderfully. We want you to aim high when it comes to your love life, and this chapter will help you score a winner.

Bad, Bad, Bad, Bad Boys Won't Make You Feel So Good

Before we start analyzing the boys you are dating, we need to talk about the types of men that a Hot Chick should never date. These men will give you nothing but drama and complications and sap the energy you should be using to love the boys who deserve it. Avoid these men at all costs, or we're pretty sure you'll only end up on *Jerry Springer* (or worse).

Boy Baddie #1: Relatives

We know you have a giant crush on at least one of your cousins. And we know you've done the research and learned that the risks of birth defects aren't actually as high as most people think. (We've done our research, too.) But even if your babies will be perfect, we're pretty sure your mom won't be so thrilled to hear that you're boinking her sister's son, and your grandma will be horrified to attend the wedding of two of her grandchildren. There are other guys out there who are just as cute and funny as your cousin and will make your family proud, so stop wasting energy climbing the family tree.

Boy Baddie #2: Polygamists

We're pretty sure that those of you who are into this kind of thing aren't reading this book, but just in case some hard-core Mormons accidentally picked it up, we want to tell you to stop it. You are a Hot Mormon Chick and you deserve to be loved by a man who loves you and only you! Please don't fall for this polygamist crap, no matter how much fun it seems on *Big Love*. Find yourself a man who wants only you, and we promise you won't go to hell for it.

Boy Baddie #3: Jailbirds

You deserve a man who can sleep next to you at night, not someone you can only communicate with through letters and conjugal visits. We know you believe he's innocent or a changed man, but we want you to find someone you can trust 100 percent, not someone who has to check in with his parole officer on your first date.

Boy Baddie #4: Your Friends' Exes

We don't care how cute he is—this is a big no-no! There are so many fish in the sea, and you do not need a fish that has already been hooked and cooked by a Hot Chick that you care about. We know there may be a few exceptions—please do not e-mail us about how you fell in love with your sister's ex-husband and the whole family is cool with it. Good for you. But in general, this is a terrible idea and it makes you a pretty terrible friend. Leave these boys alone and go get your own!

Boy Baddie #5: Your Exes' Friends

We know it's very tempting to hook up with your ex-boyfriend's best friend, either because you've always wondered what he'd be like in bed or because of the revenge factor. But this will not end well, and sleeping with someone for revenge will not make you feel great in the long run. This behavior is tacky, breeds jealousy, and won't last.

Boy Baddie #6: Your Brother's Friends

Why can't you venture out into the world and find a boy by yourself? Do you really need your brother to bring them home for you? This is a bad idea. Your bro may have the hottest friends on the planet, but he does not want to think about one of them banging his little sis. And what if you break up? Your brother won't want to hear about what a jackass his best bud is. Skip the drama and find your own man.

Boy Baddie #7: Your Parents' Friends

We don't care how hot Richard was on *Friends*—you should not be dating your parents' friends, or anyone their age, for that matter. We would feel so sorry for your daddy if he had to picture his golfing partner feeling up his little girl, so do us a favor and spare him this Greek tragedy nightmare.

Boy Baddie #8: Your Boss

We mentioned this earlier, but we can't talk about men to avoid without mentioning your boss one more time. We don't care if you actually love him (or think you do); sleeping with your boss will only make you look and feel like a gold-digging whore. If you are seriously *that* in love with your boss, find another job and *then* start boinking him, and at least he won't have to live in fear of a lawsuit for the rest of your courtship.

Boy Baddie #9: Your Assistant

You may not realize it, but this is just as stupid as sleeping with your boss. Why would you want someone who has control of your calendar and contact list to see you naked? This road leads straight to awkward town with no stops in between. Save yourself the trip.

Boy Baddie #10: Your Student

We sincerely hope you're not one of these high school teachers with a crush on a pimply fifteen-year-old student. These women are actually sick, and we don't mean to make light of this, so don't emulate those chicks on TV who claim to be truly in love with their former student. If you are a teacher, let sex be one lesson he doesn't learn from you.

Male Vibrations

Okay, now that that's out of the way, we can move on to the boys you might actually end up dating. Well, they're not perfect either. We want to be clear about the fact that we love boys. We absolutely adore every manly inch of them. But, wow, sometimes they can be problematic, can't they? Even the good ones can sometimes have absolutely no clue about how to treat a woman or even how to behave in the presence of a woman. Some of them have no idea how to treat *anyone*, including themselves. Just like us Hot Chicks, many men have fucked up♥ vibes, too. And what is worse about a boy with a bad vibe is that men are about 90 percent less likely to admit that they have a problem. (These are unscientific statistics.)

When you're out there fishing for your prize, you need to pay close attention to the vibes guys are sending out. By simply spotting a man's vibe, you'll often learn everything you need to know about him. Some of these vibes may be total deal-breakers for you, but there may be some of these icky vibes that you can live with. They may just be something for you to notice and then dismiss. Our man isn't perfect. He has his share of fucked up♥ vibes, but we love him anyway, and we aren't perfect either. So explore these vibes with an open mind and pay close attention to the ones that feel familiar. You'll learn a lot about boys and you may just learn something about yourself, too.

Ten Fucked Up♥ Male Vibes (and How to Deal with Them)

The Childish Vibe

Symptoms:

This Peter Pan–acting mo-fo just doesn't want to grow up. He may have a job (and we hope he does), but this dude will do anything and everything to avoid being a responsible adult. This guy may say things like, "I'm thirty-four, but everyone tells me I look twenty-four." If he doesn't live with Mom and Dad, then he probably has at least one male roommate who suffers from the same problem. He plays video games every single night and enjoys ridiculous, dangerous hobbies on the weekends (like blowing stuff up or bungee jumping after seven vodka and Red Bulls). This guy uses sheets as makeshift curtains and doesn't even bother to hide his porn before you come over. He will date anyone who is convenient—neighbors, co-workers, or his roommate's friends. We admit, this guy may be very, very good in bed, but be warned that if something unexpected happens (like you accidentally get pregnant), he will be zero help. Plus, we don't think he remembers the last time he washed his sheets.

Advice:

A pinch of Childish Vibe can be kind of fun. However, if you are looking for a stable and nurturing relationship, dating a guy with major childish behavior can be problematic. This guy can be a great boyfriend if you are in the same place in your lives, but we recommend someone a bit more "together" for those Hot Chicks who are Waiting to Wed.

The Frat Boy Vibe

Symptoms:

This guy isn't necessarily in a fraternity and not all frat boys have this vibe. We are talking about a guy who acts like a total meathead all the time. These boys usually talk about their sexual conquests—a lot—and not just to their bros, but to *you*. On a date! This guy usually spends a ton of time at sports bars and actually gets really emotional, moody, and sometimes violent if his team doesn't win. Men with major Frat Boy Vibe usually don't have girlfriends for very long—mainly because Hot Chicks get sick and tired of hearing about all the notches on his belt and fed up with competing for his attention during football season. Again, these guys may be really good in the sack, but you can bet that the moment you leave in the morning, he'll be on the phone with his bud describing every detail of your boobs as well as your blowjob skills.

Advice:
We have friends like this and they are a blast to have a beer with during March Madness, but dating them can be really annoying. If you are just dating to date, then go ahead and have fun doing Jager shots on Super Bowl Sunday with one of these dudes, but if you are looking for something more, it may be tough going. All that talk about all that sex he had before you is a giant red flag♥— and not because you want a virgin, but talking about how many cheerleaders he screwed in high school is actually a sign of some major LSE♥ that may leave you feeling like you're just another girl for him to add to his list of conquests.

The Supermodel Vibe
Symptoms:
We're talking about that average-looking guy who claims he only dates models. These are dumpy, short, stupid men who will only go out with a Giselle equivalent and would turn down a date with someone like Tyra. This man was born on a high horse. He thinks it's okay to call women fat, ugly, or "butter-face," and if he ever does manage to get a girlfriend, the first words out of his mouth will be, "She used to model when she was younger," or "She used to be really hot when we started dating." If you date this guy, he will

probably offer to buy you plastic surgery as a "gift" or encourage you to dress like a whore. He wants arm candy, pure and simple.

Advice:

Unless you actually *are* a supermodel, we don't suggest putting too much energy into this guy. In fact, we don't advise it for anyone. He is not someone you want to crush on. Even though you are a Hot Chick and you know it, this "I only date the prettiest girl" bullshit will probably bring out your LSE♥. We think this vibe is very unattractive. This guy does not respect women very much and has unattainable high standards for everyone but himself. We prefer men who know how lucky they are to have us and who even love our little cellulite patches.

The Scared Vibe

Symptoms:

We feel sorry for this boy because he is just scared shitless of the world. He's too timid to ask for the bill, too nervous to order an appetizer, and way too petrified to kiss you or ever grab your boob or anything fun like that. This guy probably got beaten up on a regular basis in high school, didn't get laid until he was twenty-five, and definitely didn't have any older brothers to help him with the ladies. He may be the sweetest guy on the planet, but you'd never know it because he's usually too shy to even ask you out. The Scared Vibe is often mistaken for the Dateline to Catch a Predator Vibe, which is really, really unfortunate for this dude.

Advice:

These boys are tough to get to know because they let their LSE♥ stop them from revealing their true personality. However, if you do find this guy attractive and you can figure out how to not let his severe nervousness gross you out, then you might be able to have

R P L Regina Public Library

a good relationship with him. If you like to take charge and wear the pants, this guy might be perfect for you. Maybe there's a big heart and a raging sex drive underneath all that fear.

The LSE♥ Vibe
Symptoms:

All men and women with fucked up♥ vibes have a twinge of LSE♥. LSE♥ is the root of all evil. However, the actual LSE♥ Vibe is when a boy lets his LSE♥ control his entire life. LSE♥ guys are known for dating girls who treat them like shit. They just don't have the balls to stand up for themselves and demand the respect they deserve. These guys are often totally cool and funny and smart, but they don't believe it! These guys actually need to read this book, too. They need someone to tell them they are hot, and they deserve a great relationship with a woman who loves them.

Advice:

If you find yourself with an LSE♥ guy, you should try and make him feel good about himself. He really just needs someone to kiss him all over and tell him that he's cute and funny and smart. Sometimes LSE♥ can be so strong that it's totally debilitating and makes a man lose every ounce of attractiveness. If that's the case, you need to move on to a different boy. This extreme LSE♥ dude will not be able to love you properly if he can't even love himself. But a sweet man who's never believed that he could date someone like you could become a great boyfriend once you bring out his confidence and convince him that you're lucky to have him, too.

The I'm Too Sexy Vibe
Symptoms:

Ew, gross. We hate this guy. This guy acts like the whole freaking world revolves around him and his shiny car. This boy usually only hits on girls who he thinks are a tiny bit beneath him, because he wants to be the pretty one in the relationship. He rarely compliments anyone else, but he fishes for compliments like Brad Pitt in *A River Runs Through It*. A guy with this vibe spends way too much time at the gym, waxes or shaves his body, and spends some serious time in the tanning bed. He only eats egg whites and boiled chicken and complains that he's fat if he drinks too many beers. Oh, news flash—this guy is usually not that good in bed. Guys who have to act all hot and sexy all the time usually don't have a whole hell of a lot going on in their boxers.

Advice:
We can't give you any advice on how to deal with these guys because these men repulse us. We stay far away from them. If you are into very metro, super-conceited guys, go ahead and have fun dealing with his vanity. Just try to remember that *you* are the Hot Chick in the relationship, even if he does spend five times more than you on highlights and wrinkle cream.

The Stalker Vibe
Symptoms:
This guy will call you at least three times a day, send way too many text messages, and act like a complete asshole if you reject him. Even if your grandma is *actually* in the hospital, he will try to talk you into a date and weasel his way into your night. This guy will not take no for an answer. If you tell him you don't want to see him ever again, he'll suddenly get a membership to your gym and stare at your ass while you're on the treadmill. If you date him, he might get weirdly jealous at a very inappropriate time, like on a second date. He may try to beat up the waiter because he caught him sneaking a peek at your cleavage. Guys with Stalker Vibe will also try to move your relationship forward at the speed of light.

After your first date he might show up at your apartment with groceries, make himself a sandwich, and turn on the game.

Advice:
There's no letting this guy down easy, so just be crystal clear when "dumping" him. Say, "Jack, I am not interested in you and I never will be, so stop wasting your time stalking me. It is not only scaring me, but it is also making me hate you." If that doesn't work, get a restraining order, or at least threaten to.

The Bulldozer Vibe

Symptoms:
This guy will just mow you down, slobber all over you, and talk incessantly until you have a giant case of OWL Syndrome♥. He may be overly romantic, overly aggressive, and/or overly gushy. He may try to feed you grapes or write you a song in a superficial attempt to be romantic. This guy will also try to bend you over the hood of his car on the first date, and if that doesn't work, he may still try to put his hand down your pants when he drops you off at the end of the night. A guy with Bulldozer Vibe never pays attention to how you are feeling, what you are thinking, or if you even like him. This guy has zero shame. He just goes for whatever he wants whenever he wants it.

Advice:
A teeny, tiny smidgen of Bulldozer Vibe can be hot, because a guy who takes charge in the bedroom has a touch of Bulldozer in him. The difference is that bad Bulldozer guys aren't paying attention. They'll mow you down in the middle of an excruciatingly awkward date, while a guy with the right amount of this vibe will actually notice if you two have chemistry. If you are on a date with a negative Bulldozer, say something like, "Taylor, you're moving a

bit fast—let's get to know each other and see if we have enough sparks for this kind of romantic gesture." If he bulldozes right over the hint, then get out of there before he can reveal the portrait of you he painted prior to your first date.

The Tortured Vibe

Symptoms:

Sigh. The Tortured Vibe can be extremely seductive. This guy may have actually had a hard life, or he might just get easily overwhelmed and need little old you to kiss his tears and make the world feel like a safer place for him. But the problem with tortured guys is that they usually have serious baggage. His dead daddy not only made him vulnerable, but actually may have fucked him up. He might have trouble with commitment, an inability to trust, and quite possibly a lot of anger that's making him sexy as hell but also impossible to get close to. If your date spends a lot of time at cemeteries, throws dishes at the wall in random fits of rage, or goes on a lot of trips by himself to places like Alaska, he most definitely has a Tortured Vibe.

Advice:

We know that you want to help him. We've been there. If he's open to your help and opens up to you about why he's so tortured, then that's great. That relationship might actually work. But we have to tell you that if he has a Tortured Vibe and a giant wall up and he never, ever talks to you about his past, then you will never get through to him. This relationship will never go anywhere, and guys with Tortured Vibe will often never commit, anyway. He knows that his Tortured Vibe is sexy, and we promise that you're not the first Hot Chick to find it so irresistible. Guys with this vibe are usually amazing in bed, which makes it even harder to kick these poor, wounded puppies to the curb. But we promise that if you do, you'll find someone else who is just as hot as him but will be able to open up and let you love him.

The Gay Vibe

Symptoms:

No, we're not gonna talk about guys who talk with their hands, lisp, or have sex with other men. Those men are gay and you shouldn't date them. However, guys with the Gay Vibe are "gay straight men" who are into things like bow ties, cream puffs, and throw pillows, but are actually heterosexual men.

Advice:

The trick here is to pay very close attention. If you look hard enough, it will be clear that this guy is straight. There will be something about the way he looks you in the eye or his body language that lets you know he really likes the female anatomy. There is actually something sexy about guys with a bit of this vibe, because they are comfortable in their own skin and make you feel at ease in their presence. So if you are willing to let your man plan your wedding and won't get pissed if your friends whisper to each other about whether or not your new boyfriend is gay, go ahead and date a guy with the Gay Vibe. We have a sneaking suspicion that he'll be shockingly good in bed—with a woman.

Where Are His Balls?

As you date around, you will notice that a lot of men not only have fucked up♥ vibes, but many of them are not properly wearing their balls. We encountered so many men who were acting weird in a way that had nothing to do with vibes, and one day we realized that these guys had all misplaced their balls. And where they left them revealed quite a bit about why they were acting so strange. If your man isn't wearing his pair, is wearing them crooked, or just flat out lost them, this will severely impact how he will love you. You want a man who has his balls strapped on tightly, right? You want a man who doesn't give a flying f-bomb about anything but loving you and respecting you in the right way. You want a man who is confident and self-assured and who doesn't let his LSE♥ dictate his life. Well, ladies, a man with this kind of awesomeness is a man who proudly sports his balls and never, ever takes them off.

So if your man is acting a bit off, check each of these places for his missing balls. It may not be too late to reattach them permanently.

#1: In His Desk Drawer at Work
It is very common for guys with BMS♥ to leave their balls at work. So many men are totally clueless when it comes to love and relationships, but are total rock stars at the office. These guys usually hide behind their big, fancy jobs. They tiptoe through life acting totally LSE♥, but as soon as they get to work in the morning, they unlock their desk drawer, attach their set, and take on the world with a power and strength that would be so awesome if only they used it in bed with you.

#2: In His Mom's China Cabinet

This is the ultimate mama's boy. His mother was so overbearing and protective that as soon as her baby boy turned eighteen, she detached his balls and put them in the sugar jar in her old-fashioned china cabinet. This poor guy just can't seem to get it together and meet a girl or love a girl or keep a girl. This dude will compare every girl he dates to his mommy and might end up dating someone who is really bitchy to him. If you meet a man whose mom has his twosome, take that as an ultimate red flag♥. In-laws are tough enough as it is. It would really suck if your mother-in-law was in charge of your husband's sack.

#3: In His Ex-Girlfriend's Messy Purse

This is the worst. You meet a guy who's all sweet and sexy and cool and smart, and then on the first date you realize that his ex-girlfriend has removed his balls and is carrying them around while she's moved on and is banging other blokes. Meanwhile, your date's globes are stuck at the bottom of her purse, covered in gooey lip gloss, with old gum wrappers stuck to them. We just want to shake this guy and say, "You could be so cool! Why are you living in the past and letting this bitch have all your power?" It's very hard to love a man who's letting his ex dictate his present relationship, so be on the lookout for these guys.

#4: In His Night Stand

This is the boy who's totally LSE♥ in every aspect of his life *except* the bedroom. He can't seem to hold down a relationship and doesn't know how to treat a girl in public, but if you get him into bed, he's like a knight in shining armor. We don't really understand this guy. Maybe sex is just his favorite thing ever, or maybe it's the only thing that he knows he's good at. If you meet a man who's keeping his balls next to his condoms, then have fun in the sack with his sack, but don't expect much else from him.

#5: In His Car

The guy who is keeping his balls in his glove compartment is probably confusing the hell out of you. He seems like he likes you, and then he seems like he doesn't. You go out with him once and it's amazing, you see him again and he's weirdly LSE♥, and then you see him a third time and he's super cool again! But then you have a painfully awkward phone call with him. What this means is that he keeps his balls in his car and sometimes he forgets to put them on, and other times he remembers and straps them on tightly. He might just have a really bad memory or perhaps a giant case of OWL Syndrome♥ that distracts him.

#6: In His Wallet

Two kinds of guys do this—the man who loves his money so much that he'd actually like to have dirty sex with hundred dollar bills and who flaunts his money to impress women in an extremely obnoxious manner, or the man who counts every single penny, who is frugal to the point that it makes you want to vomit, and who complains about the price of everything. These guys are very different, but they both have their poor balls flattened in their wallet, which makes it very hard for them to ever focus on a woman.

#7: In His Frat House

Guys who keep their balls at their frat house are totally LSE♥ about girls, sex, and relationships until they're hanging out with their buddies. These guys would never hit on a girl without a wingman, but act like hot shit around their bros. He'll spew cheesy pickup lines, high five his friends after making a crude comment about your ass, and send you a shot of tequila from his end of the bar. But he'd never have the balls to ask you on a proper date. It would be impossible, because his balls are under some pizza box on the floor, surrounded by his buddies, and he can't even get to them.

#8: In His High School Locker
This is the boy who lives in the past and has given his previous accomplishments all of his power. Have you ever been on a date with a guy who can't stop talking about when his basketball team won state or how he was a starter on the varsity team his freshman year and he could've been drafted into the NBA, but he hurt his knee and his mediocre life is all thanks to a torn ACL? We wish these guys would put away their yearbooks and bring their twosome back to the present.

#9: He Never Had Them
Unfortunately, some men are simply born without balls. It's not their fault and it's not their poor mothers' fault, either. These guys are just never able to get it together. They walk around life confused, unhappy, and unable to properly love a woman. There's nothing inherently wrong with these men, yet they can't commit, rarely sleep around, and will settle for pretty much anything they can get. They just drift along and only really date when a woman straps on *her* pair and asks them out.

#10: He's Wearing Them, But He Forgot They Were There
Once in a while, a man has his twins strapped on tightly but no recollection of putting them on. A man like this acts LSE♥ and usually waits for a woman to make the first move, but once a girl sees firsthand that he's wearing his balls and reminds him, he starts behaving. These guys are hard to pin down, but once you do, they make fantastic boyfriends or husbands. They just need a Hot Chick around to point to his balls every now and then and say, "See, honey, they're still there!"

Boys Need Love, Too

Despite all of our joking around about male vibes and missing balls, we really do have a huge appreciation and respect for boys (and their balls). Women spend so much time crying over men, and we simply want to help you laugh about them instead! But now we want to talk about the other parts of a boy—his heart, mind, and soul.

Men are truly just as LSE♥, sensitive, and needy as us women, and it is very important for us to love and nurture our men. They deserve to be treated with the same love and respect as every one of you Hot Chicks. They need to know that they are hot, too, and to feel just as treasured and desired and admired as you do. Many women forget this. They will date a man or even marry him and never tell him how handsome or sexy or wonderful he is. We actually know some Hot Chicks who have admitted to never, ever complimenting a man in their lives. That's totally shitty, ladies! You want your man to tell you that you're beautiful and admire your body, and he needs to hear the same encouraging words. Just like us ladies, most men have at least one thing that they are totally LSE♥ about—like their hairline, job, or height. If you know that your man feels a bit LSE♥ about something, we think it is your responsibility to make him feel amazing—or at least to try.

This is hugely important when you are in a relationship and also when you're dating. We mentioned this before, but when you are out in the dating world, you should make the guys you are dating feel good. They are nervous to be out with a Hot Chick like you, so make sure to soften things with compliments. When we met our man, we told him how hot and cute and sweet he was and what a rock star in bed he was, and he revealed that no other woman had ever told him those things. None of his exes had ever made him feel good about himself, and we're sure this is the case for tons of guys.

We're not saying to constantly gush, lick your man's feet, and worship the ground he walks on. We are talking about simple, sweet, genuine words that will make him feel loved. Don't you want him to walk out the door in the morning feeling special and loved? Well, you should, and you should make him feel that way, too. Think about this—a lot of men cheat because the other woman makes them feel more special than their girl-friend of wife. We're not trying to threaten you, but there's something in it for you if you give your man all of the lovin' he needs at home.

Don't Treat Him Like Your Bitch

We do not understand why some women put their man down in public or insult him to their friends. We think this is so low, unnecessary, and just downright ugly! We see some of you Hot Chicks snap at your guy for no freaking reason. We're not talking about PMS snapping—that is completely excusable. We are talking about women who constantly complain about their man, roll their eyes at everything he says or does, and generally make him feel like an annoying five-year-old.

We assume this is some form of LSE♥—subconsciously, these women want to make their men feel so low that he thinks he can't possibly live without them. Then these ladies feel secure that their man will never leave them. But this is a huge mistake that we don't want you Hot Chicks to make. Making your man feel like shit will only make him resent you and will only make you look like a naggy bitch. If your man has actually done something wrong, then go ahead and get mad at him, but don't act like his mere existence annoys the very crap out of you. We sincerely hope that you actually like your man, and if so, you should act like it.

Boys Will Be Boys

Although we have spent a lot of time in this chapter dissecting a man's balls and his vibes, we want to remind you not to always overanalyze your man in real life. Boys will often get moody, insecure, emotional, emotionless, crass, scared, and all sorts of nonsense. And it's not always because they are fucked up♥ or don't have their balls—sometimes it's just because they are human! We don't believe that men and women came from different planets. We're all basically the same deep down inside, but that doesn't mean that all people handle situations in exactly the same way.

So when you are out in the dating world or having trouble with your man at home, don't always pick apart every little thing he says or does. This will only drive you crazy in the long run. If he is a good guy and treats you well, you're going to have to let a few annoying things slide. That's just life, girls. He might irritate the crap out of you once in a while, and confuse you so badly that you'll want to tear your eyelashes out, but you have to pick your battles as carefully as you picked this man to begin with. Constant bickering and fighting and scrutinizing this or that aren't good for anybody. Don't ever let a man treat you badly, but know the difference between being annoying and being unkind. The point is—even the most perfect man out there will act like a complete dickhead sometimes, and that's okay. Admit it—you act like a female dickhead sometimes and so do we. Nobody's perfect, so don't expect a boy to be. Just expect him to be a human who treats you with the love and respect you both deserve.

Chapter 7

Fall in Love

EVERY WOMAN IN THE WORLD DESERVES TO FALL IN LOVE. Some of you who have never been in love before might be tempted to skip this chapter because it's too painful to read about blissful love right now, but you really shouldn't do that. It will happen. We promise. If you've built your boyfriend like we told you to and followed all of our dating advice, your Prince Charming is on his way. Now he may be in China or something, and it may take a while for him to get here, but trust that you will find the love that you deserve. And once you get it, you'd better be ready, because as wonderful as love is, it can be a big ass bitch sometimes.

We wanted to write that being in love is like being on drugs, but we didn't want people to think that we do drugs. To be clear, we don't do drugs. Anyway, love is euphoric and exhilarating, but it also makes strange things start to happen. There are dramatic highs and equally powerful lows. It feels amazing but can also cause tremendous worry and anxiety. And all of that is totally normal. Everyone gets nervous and jerky when they fall in love, but we've seen some women go so far as to fall madly in love and then completely destroy it because they let their LSE♥, OWL Syndrome♥, and bad vibes get the best of them. Well, we don't want this to happen to you. It would really suck if you worked so hard to find love and then you let it slip through your pretty little fingers because you didn't know how to handle it. So in this chapter, we are going to give you all the tricks and tips you'll need to handle every free-falling moment.

Love Laws

Falling in love is beautiful and amazing, and we want you to enjoy every succulent second of this remarkable time in your life. Some people may say that there are no rules when it comes to love, but we think that's just silly. When we fell in love, we wanted to throw all rational thought out the window, but we actually needed some guidance! We needed a girlfriend to help keep us in check and give us permission to enjoy our euphoric state. We want to be that girlfriend for you. Follow these eight laws of love so that you can bask in this awesome time without a fear or care in the world.

L: Let Yourself Fall

If you feel it happening, just totally let yourself fall off the face of the Earth in love with this dude. Don't fight it, don't analyze it, and don't stress about it. Just let go of all your LSE♥ and hop on the joyride. It may be a roller coaster of emotions for you, but don't be scared. Take your hair down, kick your fears to the curb, and just let yourself fall! You have so much more to lose if you don't.

O: Obey Your Feelings

We don't mean to be a downer here, but we know many girls who secretly know deep down that they are in love with the wrong guy. Listen to your gut. If you know this is not meant to be or won't last, save yourself a lot of time and even worse heartbreak, and start getting over him now.

V: Verify with Him

It's not that we don't trust you, but we've seen this happen, so we have to mention it. When you are falling in love, please make sure that he is falling in love, too. We are not talking about lust or infatuation here, ladies. We are talking about good, old-fashioned love. We don't want you to end up heartbroken over some dickhead whose heart and mind are not in the same place as yours, so check with him. Don't be afraid to ask him about his feelings. You need to make sure you are on the same page before you let him totally have your heart.

E: Entrust Your Heart

Once you are both on the same loving page, we want to give you permission to let him have your heart. In order to fully love, you have to fully trust. You can't be scared of this. You have to just go ahead and trust this guy with your heart. If you're keeping half of your heart for yourself just in case it doesn't work out, you're not totally giving this love a fair shot. Trust him and trust yourself. You picked him, and we're sure that if you've followed all of our advice, this dude is worthy of your trusty little heart.

L: Let Go of Toxins

When you are falling in love, you absolutely must, must, must get rid of anything and anyone in your life that could possibly interfere with you and your new man. This means you have no more long chats with your ex-boyfriend who's still in love with you, you change your MySpace profile and your Facebook profile and any other profile you may have from "single" to "in a relationship," and you tell your jealous friends and needy family members that they have to share you. When you are truly in love with someone, he should be a priority. We're not saying that you need to spend *all* of your time with him and drop everything else in your life, but we do want you to devote yourself to your relationship so that it can thrive.

A: Acknowledge His Life

Just because you're in love, that doesn't mean that life stops. You will still have work, family, and friend obligations. And guess what? So will he! Even if he's madly in love with you, he will still want to go hang out with his buddies or have to go on a work trip or spend the holidays with his own family while you go home to yours. Don't get your feelings hurt and make a foonge face♥ when real life comes calling. Just let him have his space, encourage him take care of other priorities in his life, and we promise that he'll be back in your bed in no time.

W: Welcome Honesty

Love and honesty go together like peanut butter and chocolate— if you have one without the other, it's just not quite as magical♥. Many Hot Chicks make mistakes here. They demand that their new man is honest with them, but they don't completely reciprocate. Or sometimes they spill their guts and then get all huffy when their new lover divulges a secret truth about himself. We want you to remember to step up to the plate and be honest when you are falling in love. Tell him the truth and make him feel comfortable and safe so that he'll be honest with you. If you can't trust each other, this blissful time in love will be sweet, but short.

S: Say it!

Ladies, you do not need to wait for him to say those three magical♥ words! If you are truly falling in love and keep saying "I love you" with your eyes, then just throw caution to the wind and say it with those lips. We know you're scared, but if you really, truly love this guy, then you are totally allowed to tell him. If you're worried that he might freak out and dump you, then that means you two are not really in love. When you truly love someone, we want you to go ahead and scream it from a mountaintop—or just pick an intimate moment and whisper it in his ear.

New Love Bliss

Now that you know the laws of love, we want you to make the most of the time you spend falling in love. Being single and falling in love are equally important parts of your heyday♥. And since we gave you a list of single experiences for every Hot Chick, we want to give you some special things to do while you are falling in love to help make it even more special. We want you to savor this blissful time, because as much as you want the lusty, romantic, moony, ogling period to last forever, it won't. This phase won't last and will change and grow into something else. So here is a list of things that every Hot Chick must do while she is falling in love. Pay attention even if you think it won't happen to you for a while so that these ideas will be fresh in your mind when it does.

Love Affair #1: Keep a Journal
We highly recommend writing every juicy moment down on paper when you are first falling in love. This is great for two major reasons. First, it makes it easy to compare your real man to your Build a Boyfriend list, which is totally fun, and second, you'll be able to look back on your journal one day after you two have been together for years. Don't worry about your carpal tunnel or your crappy spelling. Just jot down everything he does that makes you feel good, the intimate and fun little moments that you share, and details about your first few dates. One day, this will be so much fun to look back on, and it's also a great way to appreciate this magical♥ time right now.

Love Affair #2: Take a Trip
We know that most of you can't afford to jump on a private jet to

Venice and make out in a gondola with your new love. Neither can we. But you can probably find some way to get away for at least a day or three. Going out of town together is a fantastic way to get to know each other better and see a different side of each other. (Warning: sometimes that side is not so cute, but you better see if you can get through it together now.) It's also important to take a break from life to celebrate your new love. Stare into each other's eyes all night, drink cheap Champagne in bed, and delight in every inch of each other without any distractions.

Love Affair #3: Write Love Letters

We are giving you permission to act like you're sixteen. Go ahead and write love notes. Yes, you can write love e-mails and love text messages, but we want to encourage you to rewind your brain twenty years or so and write love letters. Mail him sweet cards or leave him secret notes. Tell him how you feel on paper. He will appreciate it now and it'll be fun for you both to look back on later.

Love Affair #4: Experiment

No, you don't have to do *that* if you don't want to . . . but if it sounds like fun, then why not try it? You two are consenting adults, and you're madly in love and you trust this guy, so now's the time to go for it. Do something you've always been curious about but never had the opportunity to try. We're not *just* talking about sex here, Hot Chicks! You could also go fishing or golfing with him, you could eat a hot dog and chase it with a Guinness, or you could help him rebuild his engine. But if experimenting in the bedroom sounds slightly more exciting to you, feel free to limit your experimentation to that arena.

Love Affair #5: Reminisce

When you've just fallen madly in love, it's super fun to go over and over and over how the two of you met, how awkwardly romantic your first kiss was, and how much fun that third date was. Just snuggle up with each other and enjoy feeling like the only two people on Earth. Your love is special, so before you get all used to each other and shit, spend some time rehashing every detail of your love.

Don't Freak Out

Oftentimes we think that once we fall in love, all our problems will disappear, and we'll forever be secure and content just because we have a giant loving hand to hold. (It's true what they say about hands, by the way.) The truth is that falling in love, and especially falling in love with Mr. Right, will bring up all sorts of issues that you probably didn't even know you had. After we fell in love, we started having crazy thoughts and feelings and weird fights with our new boyfriend, and luckily a wise woman reminded us that "Love brings up everything unlike itself." So that's what we want to tell all of you Hot Chicks. Isn't it totally strange and unfair that the best feeling in the world will make you feel some of the worst feelings? We think that this part of love totally sucks, but luckily (for you, not us) we've been through it, and we can help you get through the negative things that pop up from the depths of hell when you're on cloud nine with your hot new hunk.

How to Handle It Like a Hot Chick When Love Brings Up Jealousy

We were never, ever, ever the jealous type. We were secure and confident and living like Hot Chicks, and we never got weird about other girls. But guess what? As soon as we fell in love (like, for really reals), we started to feel a tiny bit green. Okay, sorry, we're totally lying. We were more like a bright, vibrant, Crayola Crayon green. We hated the idea that our new love ever had a past lover, we became borderline homicidal when other girls hit on our man right in front of us, and we cried when our man yelled, "Titties!" when he saw an actress's boobs on HBO. What's a girl to do when this shitty thing happens? Well, until they come up with an anti-jealousy pill or patch or something, we want you to follow these simple steps:

Note: Pay attention so that you can tell the difference between your own emotions and when your man actually does things to make you feel jealous or insecure. If he's being an assmunch, dump him, but if it's just your own hormones making you crazy, then read on.

Jealousy Therapy #1: Remember the Quote, Dammit!

Remind yourself that "Love brings up everything unlike itself." As soon as you know that some jealous feelings are "normal," you'll instantly feel less crazy and more validated. And feeling healthy and uncrazy can help tremendously in dissipating feelings of jealousy.

Note: Yes, we keep saying that feeling jealous is normal, but keep in mind that we're talking about normal-level jealousy. If you're stalking, spying, or similarly harassing your new love, then we're very sorry but we can't help you.

Jealousy Therapy #2: Hug It Out

Tell him why you're feeling the way that you're feeling. Remember, if you're normal-level jealous, then you have nothing to be ashamed of. So ask him to help you get over your nasty negative feelings. This can work even if you're a big old feminist and you're rolling your eyes right now. Consider the fact that it takes a strong woman to truly be vulnerable and honest. We know this may sound cheesy, but if you say to your man, "I'm feeling jealous and grossed out about blah blah blah. Hug me and tell me I'm pretty," your man should respond with open arms.

Jealousy Therapy #3: Flip It

This may sound manipulative, but we swear it's not. It is sometimes very necessary when our man is being stupid. If he cannot understand your tiny little jealousy issue, flip it on him. For example, say, "Baby, I'm not normally the jealous type, but if I told *you* that *my ex* used to like to (insert something that you haven't done with your current flame here), then you'd be super grossed out, too." Trust us ladies—he does *not* want to think about that stuff, which is why this shit works.

Jealousy Therapy #4: Look in the Mirror

When we're feeling jealous, we must always remember to take a good look and remind ourselves that we are Hot Chicks! Go back to page one and reread the Hot Chick definition if you have to, or call your best friend if you're still feeling low and confused and grossed out. But we are 100 percent sure that as soon as you start feeling like the Hot Chick you are, and once you remember how lucky your man is to have a hot piece of ass like you, all your feelings of green will fade into a glowy orgasm pink.

Jealousy Therapy #5: Don't Compete

What if your man has a million female friends and they don't exactly welcome you with open arms? Well, don't assume this is because they've all had marathon sex with your man or that they even want to. They're probably just selfish and lame and can't even be happy for their friend for having found such an awesome Hot Chick like you because they want all the attention for themselves. Don't even waste your time worrying about these bitches.

You also shouldn't compete with your man's past lovers. You're totally hotter and cooler than they are, or he wouldn't be with you right now, would he? We know how tempting it is to spend all day looking at their MySpace pages trying to determine if your boobs are bigger and if so how much bigger, but you have to get it together and break this addiction. If you can't find something more productive to do with your time, then go to the gym and let your jealousy fuel your workout.

How to Handle It Like a Hot Chick When Love Brings Up Trust Issues

Trust goes hand in hand with being in love. And that makes us wonder, can we really be *truly* in love with someone we don't trust? We don't really think so. This is probably why trust issues tend to pop up quicker than our new flame's package the minute we fall head over four-inch heels in love with someone. We need to make sure we can really trust him before we fall any harder.

Trusty Tip #1: Question It

If you're having a hard time trusting your new man, the first thing you need to do is ask yourself this question: *Is it my fear, or is it my intuition?* Once you have a solid answer to that question, you'll be on your way to handling your issues with trust without scaring your lover away. We'll break it down for you:

Is it your fear?

Are you just *afraid* that your man might cheat on you for no real good reason at all? Are you so madly in love with him that your heart breaks at the mere thought of him leaving you? Are you questioning your trust for him because deep down you're afraid that you're gonna marry someone like your father who cheated on your mother nine million times? Is this the first time you've ever really loved someone? And does it scare the shit out of you so much you're subconsciously searching for reasons to fuck it up♥? Does your new love seem "too good to be true," so you worry that he's got some hidden agenda, some evil master plan to have a Hot Chick in every zip code?

Okay, so if any of these hit home (even a little bit), then you're just a scared little girl inside and you're just *afraid* that you can't trust your man. That's okay. Just keep reading.

Is it your intuition?

Do you have an icky feeling in your tummy? Do you feel disrespected in other areas of your relationship? Does your honey do weird things like sleep over at his "buddy's house" because he was too drunk to drive and says he didn't call you for a ride because he didn't want to wake you? Does he leave the room every time he answers his phone? Does he turn off his computer monitor every time you walk into the room? Does he seem to go through tons of money and you're not quite sure what the hell he spends it all on? Does he keep you a secret from important people in his life? Do you feel, as a whole, totally uneasy and crazy whenever you and your man are not physically together?

If none of this feels even a little bit familiar, then it's probably just your fear. Yay! But if a lot of this felt like your existing relationship, then it just might be your intuition telling you that you indeed can't trust this lover of yours. Sorry. You might have to dump him.

Trusty Tip #2: Find Out Where

Now we're assuming that what's going on with you is just plain old scary *fear*. You are in love with this awesome guy, it's scaring the crap out of you, and now all sorts of trust issues are surfacing. Well, guess what happens now? Yep. More work. You have to figure out *where* these trust issues are coming from and *why* you're letting it mess with you. You can't be a Hot Chick if you're running around scared all the time, so put that thinking cap on that hot little head and let's find the root of this shit.

Past predicament

Very often the past can ruin a current relationship. Did

something bad happen to you during your childhood? Were your parents untrustworthy? Did your very first boyfriend lie to you and/or cheat on you and make you feel like a total fool, and now you're scared that it might happen again? Did *you* lie to a past lover and now you're freaking out that karma is going to come back and bite you in your tight little ass? Does your man have a shady past that makes you worry, "once a cheater, always a cheater"? If it's *past* crap that's taking you out of your current loving relationship, then take a deep calming breath, and put a little trust in us. We'll help you leave the past behind in Trusty Tip #3.

Present paranoia

Maybe you are a Hot Chick with a perfect past, and it's the *present* moment that's making your head spin with trust issues. Are married men constantly hitting on you? Are you the girl who watches all the men cheat on their wives and girlfriends at the office or on business trips? Is your hunk a head turner and it worries you that he's always getting sexy looks from other women? Are his friends completely immature and untrustworthy, so you assume that he might be too? If this sounds like you, then *present* situations have created weird trust issues for you. We're gonna help you learn how to live and *love* in the moment, even if you're in the middle of a world full of lies and nonsense.

Future fool

If your trust issues are not from the past or the present, then you're probably living your life in a time machine. Do you have self-destructive fantasy sequences ♥ about your future? Do you worry about things like, "What if I marry this guy, have four kids, and then when I'm fifty he goes through a midlife crisis and leaves me for a twenty-five-year-old? Oh no! I guess I can't trust him!" Are you so scared of one day finding out that you were a "fool" that you find yourself snooping and being paranoid for no good reason at all other than to protect yourself against what *might* happen in the future? Do you create trust issues because you worry yourself sick that one day he's going to wake up and not love you anymore? Well, ladies, you are a future fool, but we can totally help you come back to reality.

All of the above
Okay, so if you've read all of these and you think that your trust issues are coming from the past, the present, *and* the future . . . we're really sorry, but we think you should get professional help. We're not doctors; we're your girlfriends, and as your girlfriends, we have to tell you that if your trust issues are that deeply rooted and all over the place, you're gonna need to pay more than $14.95 for advice.

Trusty Tip #3: Deal With It!
Now that you've done a little bit of work and figured out *where* your trust issues are coming from, you are ready to actually stop the madness and *deal with it*. Don't get mad at us and think that we just wasted a bunch of your time, but it doesn't really matter what your trust issues are. It is important for you to *know*, but one isn't worse than any other. Life is too freaking short to let trust issues interfere with the love in your life. We want you to enjoy this time of falling in love without being distracted by negativity, and we're going to help you do just that. Now that you know why you're having this problem and where it's coming from, we're gonna tell you what you need to do to stop freaking out and start trusting!

Quiet your mind

It doesn't really matter if your trust issues stem from the past, present, or future, because they all have one thing in common—they're all in your hot little head. You are hot and smart and more powerful than you think. Any time you start obsessing over the past, you need to remember that it is called the past for a reason! It already happened. It's over. And no, that doesn't mean that it'll happen again. All it means is that you are wasting precious time and energy on old shit when you could be using it for new ways to love your man right here in the present. And if all you do is worry about the future, guess what? You might not even have a future with this guy, or *any* guy, if you don't squash those fears and get your head back in the game. Recognize that your mind is playing tricks on you. It's your *fear* that's making you hate your love instead of love your love. So please, start acting like the Hot Chick that you are and just stop all that negative brain activity.

Reverse your thoughts

Whenever you feel yourself thinking nontrusting thoughts, you need to reverse them. Remember, "To think is to create." If you think long enough and hard enough that he's gonna cheat on you because he cheated on his college girlfriend, then he probably will. We don't mean to threaten you, but think about it—if your guy feels like the jury's already come in with a guilty verdict, then he'll probably decide that he might as well get some fun out of it before doing his time. Instead, think about all of the reasons that you *do* trust him. Think about how happy and lucky you are because you get to share your life with someone as cool as he is. And most importantly, think about how much you deserve a lover who you trust.

Tell him

One of the most important things you can do for yourself, your man, your relationship, and your trust issues is to *tell* your man how much you trust him. Actually say the words, "I trust you." Say to him, "It's okay. Go to Vegas with your crazy, immature guy friends, because I trust you." Tell him, "I know we can have a beautiful future together, because I love you, I respect you, and I trust you." Words are super powerful, girls. We all know that words can hurt, but did you know that words can also heal? If you tell him your fears and how much you do trust him, your own words will heal your fears. Also, when your guy knows that you trust him, he'll be motivated to act trustworthy, so it's good for everyone involved.

Focus on your love, because it's all that matters

What you and your man have—that deep connection, intimate bond, solid friendship, passion, fun, emotion, excitement, contentment—all of that goodness is *love*, and all of that is real and tangible. All of those negative thoughts that are breaking the perfect little love bubble you have by making you not trust are not real. They are just fears in your brain. Fears are not tangible; you can't touch them or kiss them or hug them or smell them or have sex with them. So squash those silly fears and pay attention to your man, because he's real. And he really loves you. Take all that energy that was used for fear and use it for something good, something real—your love!

Umm, did you forget? You're hot!

We're just making sure you didn't forget that you are hot and sweet and smart and cool and confident. We just need to check in case you don't remember that you have the power to change things in your life that you don't like. So if you don't like having your issue with trust ruin your loving relationship, then take your hair down, smile brightly, and don't let it! If you want something to change, then you have to change something. And sometimes all you need to change is the knowledge that you are a Hot Chick and that you deserve all the love and trust in the world. Trust us—you are and you do!

Battlefield Boundaries

After you conquer all of your jealousy and trust issues, your relationship will inevitably have some issues of its own. They say a relationship without arguments is a relationship without passion, and we think they're right. If you and your man never disagree with each other, something's probably a little off. Either one of you is playing small♥ and is afraid to stand up for what you really feel, or one of you is being secretive and is so afraid you might get caught that you won't do or say anything to rock the boat. In healthy relationships, arguing and bickering are totally normal. At some point you will probably want to wring your man's neck or punch him in the face. But as long as you don't actually do one of those things, it's okay. Those thoughts and feelings are natural and happen to the best of us. It doesn't mean you don't love him.

Shit happens, Hot Chicks. You will indeed argue about where to eat, what to eat, his obsession with violent video games, your makeup cluttering the bathroom, past lovers, friends, family, work, money, attitudes, TV, sex, etc. Some of these may be big-ass blow-outs, and some will merely make you roll your eyes at one another, but words and fights can do real damage to relationships. Follow our fighting rules and before long, we'll have you in the throws of make-up sex instead of crying your heart out in the closet.

Fighting Formula #1: Choose the Right Time
Timing is indeed everything. Many fights could be avoided if you picked a better time to talk. If you know your man gets grumpy at night, don't bring shit up when he's about to fall asleep. We're not saying to always cater to him, but be smart and know when you'll get the reaction that you want out of him. Hunger also plays a

huge role in argument timing. If you're both suffering from LBS♥, it's probably not a good time to bring up that obnoxious thing his dad said. Just take a deep breath and wait for a decent time to put on your boxing gloves.

Fighting Formula #2: Get to the Point

Many of us get mad at our man about something, but instead of just telling him what upset us, we bring up nine million irrelevant things. This is a giant waste of time and prolongs so many arguments. If you're mad about how he told his buddies that Scarlett Johansson was the hottest girl alive, just tell him that. Don't yell at him about his dirty underwear, the toilet seat, or say that you wish he made more money. Stick to the point and say what's on your mind so that you can fight about it and move on.

Fighting Formula #3: Be Honest

We know that some of you ladies in love would rather bury what's bothering you than rock the boat. But if you keep letting things slide, you will probably end up resenting him. You are a Hot Chick. You are confident and you are not afraid to say how you feel or to demand respect. Be honest about what you're feeling and don't be afraid to fight for your own needs.

Fighting Formula #4: Listen Up

Sorry, but you're not perfect either. We know how much it sucks to be wrong, but if your man tells you something that's bugging him, do not dismiss it. Play by the golden rule♥ and admit how angry it would make you if he dismissed your feelings. So if he claims that your tone of voice upset him, simply apologize for hurting him and do your best to watch it. You'll both move on from that fight a lot faster if you own up to your own behavior. And hopefully he'll take his cue from you and take the heat the next time he fucks up♥!

Fighting Formula #5: Remember the Power of PMS

This may sound silly to some of you, but we know many of you Hot Chicks can totally relate. PMS is a real condition that can mess with your hormones and get your emotions and moods all out of whack. (If this doesn't happen to you, then we're extremely jealous.) It can be so tempting to pick the same fight every month, but we want you to stop and think about whether or not that fight is worth it. If it's legit, go ahead and battle it out when the red tide is over and you're feeling more stable. But if you know deep down that you are in a rage for no reason, then take a breath, a walk, a bath, or a Midol, but please don't take it out on your man.

Fighting Formula #6: Keep Your Hands to Yourself

We don't care how mad you are or how nasty your argument is getting—you must never hit, punch, scratch, bite, or push. If your fights are so bad that you and your man "get physical" with each other, then something is really wrong. It's not okay for him to lay a hand on you during a fight, and the same goes for you and your hands. If you can't control yourself, head to anger-management class and hang out with Naomi Campbell, but don't ever let your relationship spiral into violence.

Fighting Formula #7: Don't Say Mean Things

Even when you are in the heat of a battle, do not spit off mean, hateful, hurtful things. Saying cruel things during a fight can completely destroy a relationship. Just because you're mad doesn't mean you're allowed to call him names, be disrespectful, or say things that you know will wound him to the core. That will only keep him from trusting you. You know where the line is, ladies, so fight about what you're fighting about and don't dare cross it.

Fighting Formula #8: Don't Attack

We know that some of you Hot Chicks are spicy and fiery and have a fuse shorter than Russell Crowe, but you gotta keep that shit in check. If you're upset about something, count to ten and tell him about it from a place of love. When you scream and yell and moan and act like a total bitch, he doesn't hear what you're actually saying. He just shuts down. If you want him to care about your fight, you have to fight in a caring way.

Fighting Formula #9: Get Over It

If you've had the same fight about the same thing nine times and he's apologized sincerely, then you have to let it go. We know how hard it is to do this, but at this point the fighting isn't productive anymore. If the image of his ex-wife's face keeps popping up in your head, you can tell him and ask for his support, but don't keep screaming at him for reminiscing about her if he's already apologized. That will just make you both mad all over again and the fight will never end.

Fighting Formula #10: Pick Your Battles

Yeah, we know this is a cliché, but we couldn't write a whole long section about fighting in relationships without bringing it up. It's actually really good advice. Sometimes, your man is gonna do some really boneheaded shit and you're gonna think to yourself, "Is this even worth fighting about?" If the answer is no, just ignore it completely. It's actually a very powerful feeling to know you consciously chose a pleasant evening over a fight, so go ahead and try rewarding yourself for his dumb behavior by *not* fighting about it.

Chapter 8

After the Fall

DESPITE THE FEARS AND THE FIGHTING, BEING IN LOVE
IS PRETTY AWESOME. But then what? Unfortunately, after you
fall in love, there are only two possible options for the future with
this lover of yours. Either you will remain in love and grow together
and stay together forever, or you will grow apart or something shitty
will happen, and eventually you will break up. Yikes. We go to all this
trouble dating and searching for the right man, and unfortunately
there's just no way to know for sure which way the tide will turn.

The truth is that either way, it will take work. If you two stay together
forever, you will have to make an effort to keep the spark alive as
long as you both are alive. And if you break up, you will have to work
just as hard to get over it and move on with your life. Well, we can't
guarantee that your love will last forever, but we can help you get to
know yourself, love yourself, and treat yourself well, so that at the end
of the day or the end of a failed relationship, you will always feel like
a Hot Chick.

Breakups Suck

Looking for true love unfortunately means that you will probably have to go through some breakups. Breaking up sucks, no matter the circumstances. A breakup is the death of a relationship and can be just as heart-wrenching as the death of someone close to you. But despite the difficulty, ending a failed or failing relationship is essential to living and loving like a Hot Chick. Sometimes it is necessary to go through pain and heartache in order for us to learn, grow, and move on to find a better, healthier, more fulfilling love.

We could probably write a whole book about breakups (and maybe one day we will), but for now we are simply going to hit pause on all the lovey-dovey talk for a minute and give you the basics on how to deal with the awful reality of breaking up with someone you may or may not love. These thoughts and actions will work if you are the breaker or the breakee, because you need to move through the same process in every breakup situation. If you're breaking up with a lying, cheating, abusive dickhead or being dumped by an angel-face for some silly reason, the steps through mourning and moving on are nearly identical. So take a cleansing breath and read on through all of the ways to get over the fact that "Breakups Suck."

B: Believe in Yourself

Yes, we are going to remind you again that you are a Hot Chick! You are confident and smart and you deserve the best and brightest love on the planet. If deep down inside a little voice is telling you that the man in your life is not giving you the love you deserve, please do not ignore that feeling. That is your intuition talking. This is simple—if you think that maybe you should break up with this guy, then you definitely should. Trust that you can do it and that it's the right decision, because it is. If he's the one dumping you, then you must have faith that you will be okay. Remember that everything happens for a reason. The universe♥ would not let your soul mate slip away. This guy who does not appreciate you is giving you a giant present. He is releasing you to the other men out there who will love and value everything about you.

R: Recognize the Truth

Many girls lie to themselves. They are totally unhappy in their relationships, but they make excuse after excuse for their men. Please don't do this, ladies. Be honest with yourself. If you hear yourself saying things like, "Sure, he drinks a twelve-pack every night, but he's not an alcoholic," or "He told me he doesn't love me, but I know he didn't mean it," listen to yourself and know that you deserve someone you won't have to make excuses for.

E: Educate Him

We know that breakups can be nasty, but we'd love for you to take this opportunity to help mankind. There are a lot of guys out there who have no idea how to treat a woman and never learn. If you are going through a heart-wrenching breakup, don't just call him an asshole and throw shit on his lawn, or scratch and wail and beg him to stay with you. Take the time to calmly explain why you can't be with him or why you still love him. Let him know your feelings and explain that you want to live your life with a love that is positive and invigorating and healthy. He may not listen, so you might need to just mail him a letter or something, but if this guy can learn from your breakup (like you will), then hopefully he won't be so insensitive to the next Hot Chick who dates him.

A: Analyze Your Life

Go lock yourself in your closet for an hour and really analyze your life. Think about how you feel with this man, how intertwined your lives are, and how you can make the best possible break from him that will cause the least amount of pain. Do you have the same friends? Do you live together? Do you have children? Unfortunately, you probably can't just run away. Breakups do take some planning, so make a list of the obstacles that are keeping you from kicking him to the curb immediately, and then come up with a strategy to conquer them.

If he's dumping you, then you need to take a good look at your life to see how you can move on as easily as possible. Think about how you can reorganize your life to ease the pain. It might mean hanging out with different friends, avoiding certain places where you know you'll run into him, finding a roommate and a new apartment, or even going home to hang out with your mama for a while. Remember to focus on all of the positives in your life, then get ready to step back out into the world prepared to have a fresh new heyday♥.

K: Kick Fears to the Curb

There is nothing to be afraid of, darlings. You can do this! As painful as it is, you will get through it, and one day soon you will look back on this time and smile. You will be so proud of yourself for strapping on your balls and standing up for yourself, or for not letting the fact that he broke up with you keep you down. Don't be afraid that you will now be alone and miserable for the rest of your life! Just start over from the beginning of this book and have fun being single again. That's not so scary now, is it?

U: Use Your Friends

The universe♥ made girlfriends for two reasons: for fun and for times like this. Lean on your girlfriends and listen to them. They can give you great advice because they have each gone through breakups of their own and can see your relationship from a different perspective. Go with your girlfriends to lunch, yoga, on a little girly trip, or shopping (not that we promote retail therapy or anything). And go forward knowing that you have a bunch of Hot Chicks who love you and will send you great vibes to help you conquer this shitty time—including us!

P: Plan Ahead

Whether you are dumping or being dumped, it is very important that you make a plan for your future. Get your head out of the past, quit rehashing your relationship, and stop looking through old photos. You need to move forward with organization and thoughtfulness, so take a step back and think about what you want right now. Is it a good idea to be single for a while and reevaluate what you want, or do you want to start looking for another relationship right away? Think about what didn't work in this relationship and revise your Build a Boyfriend list accordingly. Spend some time getting excited about planning your future, because if you just wander aimlessly, you may end up back in that wrong relationship or in one that's even worse.

S: Seal Up Loose Ends

We hate hearing Hot Chicks talk about how they can't move on from an old relationship because they don't have "closure." Don't waste time with this, because you may never get satisfactory answers to all of your questions or find true enlightenment about what went wrong. You can't force him to give you closure, but what you can do is your part to give it to yourself. Seal up loose ends and put your heart at ease by saying everything you need to say or writing down all your feelings. And tell yourself that you now have closure, even if he never gives you the response you want.

S: Shut the Door

Don't just close it—dead bolt that shit. Seriously. You'll never move on if you literally and/or figuratively keep the door open for this dude to come back into your life. If you two are actually meant to get back together, it will happen naturally. But first, you need to cut off communication so that you can heal and regain control of your life. Then if something serendipitous happens and you two meet back up and there are positive fireworks, then fine. But for now, no coffee dates, friendly lunches, or invitations for him to stop by. Lock the door, put the chain on, and focus on living your life like a Hot Chick.

U: Undertake Something New and Positive

Any time you're trying to break a bad habit (like smoking, drinking, or online shopping), you need to fill your time with something harmless. And so in the case of a breakup, you need to replace the guy with something positive. We highly recommend that you don't just replace him with some other randomly available penis. It's much healthier in the long run to take up knitting or cycling or something like that. We're not saying that a quick rebound fling is necessarily a bad idea—it's often a good thing to remind yourself that you are hot and desirable. But golfing and ballroom dancing are also good ways to surround yourself with cute boys while giving your heart time to heal.

C: Cleanse Your Life

You are officially allowed to keep *one* box, but that's it. Don't lie around the house in his old Giants T-shirt. Take his pictures out of the frames and off the refrigerator. Throw out his toothbrush. Then give the rest of his shit back to him. We're not saying to burn all evidence that you were ever a couple, but it is healthy to purge. You are a single Hot Chick now, and you need to set up your life and your physical space accordingly. It'll be infinitely better for your head if you don't have reminders of him everywhere you look.

K: Keep Your Heart Happy and Your Head Busy

Treat yourself extra well during this rough time. We give you full permission to indulge in all of the things in life that give you pleasure. Go ahead and balance out this crappy period with positive things you've been craving. It can be anything—chocolate cake for breakfast, a night out with your girlfriends, a massage, a new lip gloss, a few days off from work, a whole new wardrobe, flowers, or tango lessons. These things may sound frivolous, but treating yourself great right now will help make you feel a little better.

Dumping Dilemma: The Quiz

It's often unclear whether or not you should end a relationship. If you're thinking about calling it quits, then you should probably listen to those thoughts. Intuition is the bomb, Hot Chicks! But like we said before, sometimes it's hard to tell the difference between your intuition and fears. It can also be tricky to decipher what is normal relationship crap and what is downright disrespectful. Plus, it's often hard to let go of a comfortable, decent relationship, even if it's not quite what you want. If you are in a relationship and don't know if you should stay or go, pull out a pen and take our fun (but very serious) breakup quiz so that you can make a clear and confident dumping decision.

1) How often does your man compliment you?

A—All the time! He does a great job of making me feel hot and sexy and smart.

B—Not too often, but when he does it seems genuine.

C—Only on big occasions like when I'm dressed up for an event.

D—He's never really given me a genuine compliment. I do wish he'd tell me I was pretty once in a while.

2) Do you and your man have fun together?

A—We always have a great time, even if we're just at home watching TV.

B—We don't get to connect on a day-to-day basis, but when we go out together we have a good time.

C—We don't think the same things are fun. We like going out in groups, but when we go out by ourselves, usually at least one of us is bored.

D—We haven't had fun in a long time, because lately all we do is argue.

3) How often do you and your man fight?

A—We've had one or two fights and some small bickering, but we get along really well.

B—There are a few issues that we constantly fight about, but otherwise we get along.

C—Our big fights are intense blowouts and we bicker pretty often, too.

D—We fight about everything—even the way we fight! Our big fights include name-calling and broken dishes. I can't remember a day recently when we didn't fight about something.

4) Do you do sweet little things for your man?

A—Yes, I love to cook for him or surprise him or leave funny little notes in his bag. I also like to help him out when I know he's busy by doing small things like filling his car with gas or going to the post office.

B—I'm too busy to do extra things, but I do enjoy planning birthday dinners for him and stuff like that.

C—I used to, but I stopped because whenever I did something nice for him, it wasn't reciprocated.

D—I'd rather plan a special night out with my girlfriends. He'd never appreciate it, anyway.

5) How is your sex life?

A—Pretty awesome! We have passion and we love each other's bodies. We can be kinky or intimate or just laugh and have fun in bed.

B—I can't complain. It's nice and fine and we get the job done.

C—I've had better, but I've also had worse. We don't have the world's best chemistry, but at least he tries.

D—We don't do it very often, and it feels like we're losing attraction for each other.

6) Does your man do nice things for you?

A—He does at least one little thing every week that makes me feel loved and appreciated.

B—He forgets to do things like call if he's gonna be late, but then he makes up for it by sending a sweet e-mail or buying me a cupcake.

C—He gets really wrapped up in his own life and doesn't seem to have time for little things. I don't need much, but a small gesture once in a while would be nice.

D—He's cheap and lazy and would never think to do something sweet. He never really courted me and in general takes me for granted, and I'm starting to resent him.

7) In general, how does your man make you feel?

A—Like a Hot Chick! I know he loves and respects me.

B—He lets me know he cares about me, but I wish he'd make more time for me.

C—He says mean things that make me feel bad about myself,

but usually only when we're fighting.

D—Honestly, he makes me feel LSE♥. I don't think he's that attracted to me or really respects me, or he wouldn't act the way he does.

8) Which sounds like the most fun?

A—Lying naked in bed with my man and kissing him all over.

B—Relaxing on the couch with my man and watching *American Idol*.

C—Getting dressed up and going out to a club. Even if I'm with my man, it'll be nice to get looks from other guys.

D—A girls' night out when we can let loose! The only way I can really have fun is if my man's not around.

9) Does your man look at other women?

A—Once in a while he'll say that an actress or model is pretty, but he usually makes me feel like the hottest girl in the room.

B—He often talks about other girls being hot, but he always says that I'm even hotter than them!

C—His eyes follow every cute girl we pass, but I've learned to live with it.

D—He not only looks but compares me to other chicks, and it seems like he'd rather be with anyone else but me.

10) Complete this sentence: My man is. . .

A—The love of my life.

B—My best friend.

C—A decent practice boyfriend.

D—An addiction.

Scoring:

For each question, A = 4 points; B = 3 points; C = 2 points; D = 1 point.

Results:

31–40 Points: Why did you even take this quiz? We hope you can recognize a good relationship when you have one, because it sounds like you have one! It may not be totally perfect, but nothing is. It seems like you have something healthy and fun, but only you know the truth. You don't have to stay with him just because you have a ton of points. Don't settle if it doesn't feel magical♥, but we have a feeling it does.

21–30 Points: You and your man have a few areas that need improvement, but that's okay! We think you should take the time to work that stuff out, because it sounds like this relationship has lots of potential. Of course, if you know in your heart that it isn't meant to be, then let him go and move on! But we think you should give it a chance first.

16–20 Points: Oh, honey, you can do better than this. It doesn't seem like this relationship is serving you well. If you want to try to save it through counseling, then you should definitely try, but if your heart is not happy, it's time to kick him to the curb! Stand up for yourself and start working on getting that great love that you deserve

10–15 Points: You probably know it's time to break up with him, and now you have confirmation from us that it's time to break up with him. Go for it. We have your back! Just dump him! You deserve better.

A Word on Forgiveness

Even the best relationships are still imperfect, because we Hot Chicks and the men we love are all flawed. This means that a successful relationship will always require a certain amount of forgiveness. In order to stay in love with someone, it is essential for us to be willing and able to genuinely forgive. We think there are two types of forgiveness—painless forgiveness and painful forgiveness—both of which are equally important parts of staying in love.

By painless forgiving, we are talking about getting over petty little irritating things like burping and dirty underwear. We should never let these insignificant flaws get in the way of our passion, and deciding whether or not to forgive a man for these things should never even be a question. Men are human, and we have to forgive them for this in order to fully love them. We've seen so many girls hold grudges against their men for the silliest things, like eating an extra hot dog, talking louder after having three beers, or the fussy way he hangs his shirts to make sure they dry in the sunlight. Sure, these things may be annoying, but they are also normal and harmless, and they are exactly the kinds of things that need to be forgiven if your relationship is going to work. They're totally painless, and if you can't find it in your heart to forgive these things, you probably don't truly love the man who's doing them.

On the other hand, there are always going to be some things in a relationship that require much more thought and work to forgive. We call this painful forgiving, because sometimes forgiveness can be just as heartbreaking as a nasty breakup. If your man lies, cheats, or engages in some sort of behavior that compromises your relationship (like an obsession with pornography or an addiction to painkillers), it won't be easy to forgive him. And in a way, that's a good thing. When it's hard for you to forgive, that means you are rethinking what kind of love you deserve, and that is extremely important for you to do when something major like this happens. You can't just brush major things under the rug and keep forgiving your man if he is being disrespectful, unfaithful, or just a plain old dickhead. In these cases, you need to think about how his behavior makes you feel and whether or not it is something you can forgive.

Unfortunately, you will have to decide for yourself if you should forgive your man. We can't tell you what to do because only you know if you'll ever be able to truly forgive him and move on or if you'll always secretly resent him. All we can do is encourage you to take the time to figure out which is true for you. We give mad props to all of the Hot Chicks out there who can forgive major fuck ups ♥. We know (from experience, unfortunately) how painful it is and how much work it takes to get from there back to a place of unconditional love. But if you can't find it in your heart to forgive giant trespasses, that is perfectly okay, too. Forget what the Bible says: sometimes the pain is just not worth the prize. There are many cases when forgiveness is not the right decision for you or your relationship. And knowing yourself well enough to make that choice and having the self-respect to act on it are two giant steps toward loving like a Hot Chick.

Sex in Relationships

Let us start off by saying that if you are a sexually active adult and you're officially dating someone or have a boyfriend, then you should be having sex with this person. If you're exclusively dating a guy but withholding affection or intimacy, you are not acting like a Hot Chick. If you have a history of abuse or any sort of serious issue that is preventing you from enjoying intimacy, then you need to get your hot ass into therapy, pronto. You'll never be able to give or receive love until you get over it.

Dating someone who withholds sex can be very hard on men. We know too many men who stray simply because their woman never touches them or kisses them or plays with them. Some of you may be rolling your eyes and screaming, "It's not my job to get him off!" But we disagree. If you are exclusively dating a guy, then who else's job would it be? It's like Chris Rock's classic bit about Hillary: Monica never should have stood a chance because Hil should have been down there preemptively satisfying her man. Well, Chris may have taken it a bit too far, but we agree with him on this point: it is your job as a girlfriend/wife/whatever to love and satisfy your man, just like it is his job to love and satisfy you. In case you're still not sure what we mean, here are five sex don'ts for all of you Hot Chicks in a relationship:

Sex Suggestion #1: Don't Treat Sex Like a Present

We know so many girls who only give it up on their man's birthday or Valentine's Day, but we don't think they are acting like Hot Chicks. Sex is not a present. It is not a gift from you to him. Sex is something that you two should share and that you should both enjoy! If you don't enjoy it, then you've got a problem. Yes, your vagina is special, but it's not some prize that can only be won when Santa comes to town or if there is cake involved (unless you're into that sort of thing). Get off your high horse and mount your man instead!

Sex Suggestion #2: Don't Use Sex as a Weapon

This is similar to suggestion #1 but merits its own space. So many girls we know punish their men by withholding sex as if it is some kind of cookie and he's a three-year-old. If you are mad at your man about something he did, then be honest and clear with him and work through it together, but don't tell him that he's not going to be getting any until he buys you six dozen roses and brings you breakfast in bed every day for a month. That may sound like fun, but it does not sound like a healthy relationship.

Sex Suggestion #3: Don't Withhold Sex Because You're Not That Into Him

We hate girls who start dating a guy who is falling in love with her, but she purposely puts off getting intimate because she's just waiting for somebody better to come along! No, ladies, that is so fucked up♥! If you are dating a guy because you'd rather date someone than no one, this might be you. You are too LSE♥ to be alone, so you lead this poor guy on and just avoid sexy situations. Stop playing games, stop wasting his time, and do both of you a favor—either commit to dating him or commit to finding someone you actually want to have sex with. You both deserve better!

Sex Suggestion #4: Don't Treat Your Boyfriend Like Your Buddy

Some women meet a fantastic guy who they have a blast laughing and joking with, but they can't even *fathom* the idea of doing the nasty with him. Then after every fun dinner and great movie, they pull some stupid excuse out of their ass to duck out of anything romantic. Gross! Does this sound like you? Do you love everything else about your guy, and are you enjoying going on dates, but the idea of sex with him is repulsing to you? If so, sorry, but you are not being a Hot Chick. Remember that you deserve someone who you can laugh with *and* have fun in the sack with! Go have fun times with your girlfriends and stop wasting this poor man's time and money by palling around with him when you know that he wants more from you.

Sex Suggestion #5: Don't Withhold Sex Because You're LSE

Yes, we said it before and we'll say it again right now. If you are dating a guy, you have to believe that he thinks you are beautiful and sexy and perfect. You cannot say no to sex with him because you ate a cupcake at work and you're certain that it's already showing on your thighs. And you shouldn't avoid letting him see your naked body by keeping the lights off or sticking to certain positions that show you in your best light. The sex will be so much better the moment you stop thinking about that stuff and let yourself get lost in the moment. Just say to yourself, "I am a Hot Chick, hear me roar," and then go ahead and roar!

Exercise Your Love

After you fall in love (and you will, we promise), we want to help you stay there. Staying in love does take just as much time, thought, and energy as breaking up, but it's definitely a lot more fun. We haven't been married for thirty years, so we can't claim to have the secret to a perfect relationship, but the truth is that there is no secret. Just like anything else in your life, if you want to achieve success in your relationship, you need to give your relationship attention, effort, and nurturing care.

Staying in love is just like exercise. If you work your ass off at butt class♥ (literally), but then stop going and start eating a bunch of nonsense, what happens? Of course, your ass will grow back, and it will usually attach itself in a bigger, badder way. Well, the same thing goes for your love life. If you work your ass off (figuratively) to find a good, loving relationship, you can't just get all lazy and stop doing and saying all of the sweet things that made you fall in love in the first place. If you worked hard to find this love, it would be a sin to lose it due to laziness. And if you lucked out and didn't need to work so hard to find it, it would still be a giant waste to take your love for granted. We want you to love your partner and enjoy every juicy, magical♥ moment you two share. So don't get too comfortable and fuck it up♥, girls. Buck up and take your relationship to the gym!

Adoration Exercise #1: Communicate Lovingly
Open communication is essential, but it is equally important to communicate with care. Think about the way you spoke to each other when you were first dating. Don't get all complacent and start bitching and nagging; speak to him with that same adoration

in your voice. Of course, he needs to respectfully communicate with you as well, but you can set the communication standard by staying tender and positive. Also remember that touch is a form of communication. Holding hands, giving hugs, and kissing his face a million times for no reason at all does a lot for a relationship. Communicating through touch can help you stay closer connected.

Adoration Exercise #2: Argue Softly

We've already talked about fighting, but we want to remind you one more time to always do it with care. We're all gonna brawl sometimes, but in order to stay in love you must fight smartly and softly. Bite your tongue before you say something that will just lead to a bigger fight. Words are very powerful, and if you two say too many mean things to each other, it's going to be hard to get back to a place of trust and adoration.

Adoration Exercise #3: Compliment Frequently

If you want to stay in love forever, you need to tell your love how special, smart, hot, sexy, funny, and cute he is on a regular basis. We've mentioned this before and we hate to sound repetitive, but this is so important! The more you lift your man's spirits and his self-confidence with your encouraging, complimentary, honest words, the better he will feel—and the better he feels, the more adored he'll make you feel. And if you both feel adored and confident around each other, you have a pretty good chance of staying in love.

Adoration Exercise #4: Make Love Passionately

Now that you've been together for a while, don't you dare laze out and get all boring in the bedroom! Get off your back and put some back into it. Don't think about your grocery list while you give him a B.J. and don't just lie there while you're doing it waiting for him to finish. We know how busy and stressful life can get and that sometimes a good night's sleep sounds like way more fun than a hot round of sex, but force yourself to try to get into it. It's kind of like how plastering a smile on your face magically♥ makes you happy—by forcing yourself to act passionately, pretty soon you'll be feeling truly passionate.

Adoration Exercise #5: Make Time Regularly

We know that as life moves on it becomes harder and harder to find time to enjoy each other's company. Even so-called "date nights" are more stressful than they're worth with babysitters and reservations and bedtimes. So we want to encourage you to make time for each other within your routines. Cook meals together on Sunday afternoons, or take turns cooking for each other if one of you is too much of an alpha chef. Or do something simple like have a bread and cheese picnic on your dining room floor after the kids are asleep. Sometimes a relaxed night out in your own home is all you need to keep the love alive.

Adoration Exercise #6: Practice Spontaneity

Once you two settle into a lovely little routine together, it can become very hard to break that schedule. But that can often lead to boredom, so make sure to keep some level of spontaneity in your relationship. If you work near each other, surprise him by taking him to lunch, or go get a drink together after work for absolutely no reason at all. Simply changing things up can help you bust out of a tedious habit and have you falling in love all over again.

Adoration Exercise #7: Play Dress Up

We encourage every woman to spend a little time and just a little money on some very little things that will make her feel sexy. We talked about this in "Single Experiences," but it is just as important for you ladies in love. Dressing up in hot outfits or cute PJs can make you feel hotter, and when you feel hotter, soon your man and your relationship will be, too. Our fiancé recently said to us, "Sorry if I'm not turned on when you're wearing a giant robe, carrying a mug of coffee, and furiously typing away on the keyboard." (Ouch!) Well, as annoying as that was to hear, just putting on our little Victoria's Secret shorts that say PINK across the butt perked us up and helped us get a little slap on the ass when we walked by with our coffee. And it's those little things, like feeling sexy and getting slaps on the ass, that can keep a relationship strong and healthy.

Bring Back That Loving Feeling

True love is like a song. It can be sad, but it can also be uplifting, comforting, invigorating, and motivating. A song can change your mood in an instant, and being in love can do the exact same thing. It can make all the stresses of life seem unimportant, and put a smile on your face even in the worst of times.

One of our favorite love songs is "You've Lost That Loving Feeling," because it ends on such an uplifting note. It reminds us that we can bring back that loving feeling even if it seems gone, gone, gone. And it's true. If you've lost your loving feeling, we want you to bring it on back, girl. You have the keys to turn a lackluster story into some beautiful lyrics, because your love is worth fighting for. You don't find a love like this every day. So take our advice, and take a note from the Righteous Brothers, and don't let it slip away. (If you have no idea what we're talking about, then listen to Justin Timberlake and think of this as "Bringing Sexy Back.")

Step 1 to Bring It on Back: Have a Heart to Heart
If you've lost that loving feeling, but you swept it under the rug because you didn't feel like dealing with it, then we want you to pull back that dirty, ratty rug and start sweeping and polishing! You are a Hot Chick and if you're feeling unloved or unloving, then you need to take control and get your love back. Sit your man down and tell him exactly how you feel. Let him know how important your love is to you and that you want the

spice back. Let him know that you long to feel twitterpated♥ again and that you need him to work with you on making your love a priority.

Step 2 to Bring It on Back: Pull out the Memory Books
Remember the love letters and journal we encouraged you to write while you were falling in love? Well, this is one good use for them! When your love is faltering, you can dig around in your attic, pull out the old cards, notebooks, and photo albums, and have fun reminiscing. Simply taking the time to remind yourselves of how and why you fell in love and what it felt like at the time can be enough to make it happen all over again.

Step 3 to Bring It on Back: Plan a Mini-Romantic Vacation
Going away together, far from any bills and kids and dirty dishes, can do a lot to bring that spark back. We think that going on one of those all-inclusive couples' vacations is a fantastic idea, because you'll be surrounded by other loving couples and newlyweds who will mirror back to you the love you used to have. Go somewhere quiet and exciting and romantic. Leave your BlackBerries at home and just be together. It may be rough or awkward at first, but stick with it. Focus on one another until loving touch and communication comes naturally again. It's like riding a bike. You may be a little wobbly and LSE♥ at first, but after a few miles of flat road it will start to feel fun and freeing again.

Step 4 to Bring It on Back: Find a New Hobby
We want you to find a new hobby that you and your man can do together! If you're the athletic types, stop going to the gym separately and join a coed soccer league. Or if you can talk

your man into it, take dance lessons and then actually go out dancing together. If you don't feel like moving, there's always cooking classes or wine-tasting lessons or a book club. It doesn't matter what it is—just think outside the box and get your love back by enjoying something fresh and new together.

Step 5 to Bring It on Back: Go on a Retreat or to Counseling
If your lack of love is beyond the point where trips and hobbies can help, then we strongly encourage you to enroll in counseling. Just make the appointment, handcuff your man to your hip, and drag him along. But don't think for a second that you are "above" therapy. Going to therapy does not mean that you are a failure. It's quite the opposite, actually. It means you are not a quitter. It means you are determined to make every day a heyday♥ with your new love, and that makes you a Hot Chick.

We also think you should stop rolling your eyes at those cheesy sounding relationship retreats. They have retreats for engaged couples and married couples, and they are actually really worthwhile. We had to go on one of these before getting married. It was difficult and emotional and draining, but we learned a lot. Most important, we were reminded of how necessary it is to always make the decision to love. That's exactly what we're talking about here. You can ignore the problems and pretend that you are happy coexisting without passion, or you can fight for the love you deserve and decide that you are willing to do everything in your power to get it back.

Afterword

We Love You!

Ladies, we have said it over and over again, and we want to tell you one more time how much we want you to go on out there and get the love that you truly do deserve. We want your heart to be filled with so much freaking love that it pops out of your pretty little eyeballs. We know that right now it may seem impossible to ever find that level of love, but if you take one thing from this book, we hope it is the belief that you can and you will.

There are too many unsuccessful relationships out there. Too many women settle for less than they deserve because they think that they're not cool enough or pretty enough to ever find true love. And we know too many ladies who lack self-respect and will put up with abuse or zero excitement, or who will spread their legs for any man who looks in their direction. If this is you, we want you to know that as long as you live in that dark, negative, unloving cave and project LSE♥ and negativity out into the universe♥, you will continue a vicious cycle. You'll never find true love and you'll pass your poor choices onto the next generation of Hot Chicks who will never get the love they deserve, either.

But you have the power to change it right now. Flip the switch right this instant and decide that you will not settle for anything less than everything you want. We promise that it is out there, so step up to the plate and create a heyday♥ for yourself that is full of all sorts of loving goodness. You have the strength to do this, and you now have all the knowledge and the tools you need to change the way your own love story is written.

So congratulations, beauties! You have everything you need. Now all you have to do is live it! Whether you are single, dating, married, or divorced, the first step is to get your cute little ass out there and celebrate your new hot love life. If you're single, grab a girlfriend or the first cute guy you find, and if you're in a relationship, grab your man. Pop open a bottle of Champagne, eat a piece of chocolate cake if you want, and celebrate the fact that you are a Hot Chick who will absolutely get that deep, wonderful, pure, honest, passionate love that you completely and absolutely deserve.

Good luck, Hot Chicks!

We love you,
Jodi and Cerina

Hot Lingo

BMS:

This stands for Bill Merrit Syndrome. Bill Merrit is one totally gross guy we dated, but he shares an affliction with many men who also suffer from BMS. The primary symptom is when a man uses his busy, important work schedule as an excuse to shut out the possibility of love or a relationship, or even some fun crazy messy sex. Secondary symptoms include being totally LSE♥ about sex and being stingy with compliments. Men with this syndrome tend to keep their balls in their briefcase, or else they just leave them in their desk drawer and only put them on at the office. Hot Chicks do not date men with BMS.

Butt Class:

You may not believe us, but we used to have a lame, flat, white-girl ass until we got that flat ass to the gym and started taking lots of butt classes! Butt classes are also called boring things like Body Sculpting or Weight Training, but we think our term is more descriptive. Butt classes include tons of squats, dead lifts, and lunges, and we prescribe taking them twice a week for maximum butt benefits.

Fantasy Sequence:

A daydream that you purposely create, or one that just sort of happens when something or someone is in the back of your mind—your imagination runs wild and creates something totally fun. For example, you may have fantasy sequences about finally telling off that annoying chick at work who reads your e-mails over your shoulder, making out with your boyfriend in the middle of a boring meeting, or maybe just looking absolutely adorable and irresistible as you flirt with the hot barista at Starbucks.

Foonge Face:
Stems from the Italian spelling of fungi, meaning mushroom. If you look at a mushroom, the top of it curves down, looking like a little sad face. Girls with foonge faces feel sorry for themselves for no reason and walk around with grumpy looks on their faces. We encourage all you Hot Chicks to smile, knowing that you have the power to change your mood along with your reaction to anything that would give you a pouty little foonge face.

Fucked Up:
In our last book, we defined certain foods as being fucked up, but now we are using this term for something in your love life that makes you feel LSE♥, scared, miserable, extremely jealous, passionless, untrusting, or furious. You might fuck up, he might fuck up, or something in your relationship might just be fucked up, but in any case you need to deal with all of your fucked up shit in order to get the love you deserve.

The Golden Rule:
"Do unto others as you would want done unto you," or "Love thy neighbor as thyself." There are a million different wordings for the golden rule, but they all mean the same thing: *treat other people exactly how you would want them to treat you in the same situation.* Living by the golden rule is a key Hot Chick trait because it means that you are honest and thoughtful and compassionate in all of your relationships.

Heyday:
The very best, most magical, hottest time of your life—no mat-

ter what age box you check, or if you're married, single, gay, or straight. Your heyday begins when you stop having a pity party and decide that you're hot and worth all the fun in the world. You will look back one day and shake your head and giggle, remembering all of the fun, crazy, ridiculous times you had during your heyday. And it will be worth it.

Heydayish:

Our code word for when we're in the mood for some loving. Hot Chicks don't use the word "horny," and there aren't many other good options to describe this feeling, either. We're feeling heydayish when we really, really want a big giant boy to go downtown and then bake in our bed. Examples for using it in a sentence: "I only went home with him because I've been feeling heydayish," or "I'm not going out tonight because I am feeling heydayish, and I might do something stupid."

LBS:

Stands for low blood sugar. LBS is a very serious condition, even for those of us without any medical problems. The symptoms of LBS are almost identical to those of another affliction we Hot Chicks suffer from, PMS. If we go too long without food, we become snarky, miserable, and downright inconsolable. Make sure to take care of yourself and eat every few hours, or the snapping, bitching, and fighting caused by your LBS is likely to wreak havoc on your relationship.

LSE:

Stands for low self-esteem. It is a disease that infects everyone from time to time, but Hot Chicks try really hard to cure themselves of this plague. The best thing about the term LSE is that it can be used as a noun, verb, adjective, or whatever. For example, you can be feeling LSE, someone can just be LSE, or your LSE can just act up unexpectedly. LSE is *not* hot, ladies, and recovering from this deadly infection is the first and biggest step to truly being a Hot Chick.

Magic:

This is our word for something or someone that is perfectly hot, perfectly fun, or makes you feel like the happiest girl on the planet. Example for using it in a sentence: "I'm wearing my magic pants tonight," "Was your date magic?" or "Something happened, our trip was magical!"

Mary Kate:

We don't mean to seem insensitive, but we started using this term for being a little bit anorexic or just fucked up about food. It is not hot to be Mary Kate, but this term can be used in many forms, which we love. Examples for use in a sentence are, "You only ate two bites of your dinner—are you pulling a Mary Kate?" or "Did you see how grossly skinny that girl was? She's totally Mary Kate."

OWL Syndrome:

Stands for overwhelmed with life and is pronounced like the bird. OWL Syndrome can occur when you have way too much going on all at once, or if something unexpected happens (whether it's good or bad) that totally freaks you out. Examples: OWL Syndrome can take effect when your boss puts a giant folder on your desk filled with crap that she wants you to finish by 6 p.m., when you get a nasty passive-aggressive e-mail from your mother, and that cute guy you met online calls to say he wants to have dinner with you tonight at seven.

Play Small:

The origins of this term are actually from a Marianne William-son quote—"Your playing small does not serve the world. There's nothing enlightening about shrinking so that others feel secure around you." We couldn't have said it better ourselves. Hot Chicks do not play small, apologize for who we are, or act LSE♥ to make people feel better about themselves. That's not hot, and to stop playing small is a big step in living like a Hot Chick.

Red Flags:

These are warning signs—sometimes they are giant and some-times they're very subtle. Examples: A guy you're dating says to you, "I would tell you that you're beautiful, but I'm sure you hear that all the time." A little red flag should go up. This guy probably has BMS♥. Or how about when a superior in your business in-vites you to coffee to talk about future projects, and then "coffee" mysteriously turns into a candlelight dinner where he orders beef Carpaccio, a bottle of expensive vino, and buys you a rose? A *giant* red flag should go up, telling you that he doesn't want you involved in his business plan; he wants you naked in his bed.

Self-Destructive Fantasy Sequences:

These are the negative, nasty versions of fantasy sequences♥. This is when your mind latches onto something horrific and upsetting, and your imagination runs wild with it. It is not hot to indulge in these obnoxious thoughts! Don't let self-destructive fantasy se-quences happen. You are only wasting precious time and energy that could be used toward your heyday♥.

Twitterpated:

To be giddy and so overjoyed and anxious with feelings of love that it makes your heart pop out of your eyes whenever you're around your new crush. Origins: Disney's *Bambi*, when all the little animals were mating and falling in love because it was spring. Examples for using it in a sentence: "I know he's the one because it's been a year and a half and I'm still twitterpated," or "I really didn't mean to have sex with him on the first date, but I couldn't help it—I was so twitterpated!"

Universe:
The universe is a stand-in for God or fate or whatever you believe in. We Hot Chicks believe firmly that the universe loves us and takes care of us and gives us exactly what we need in its proper time. But we have a give-and-take relationship with the universe—we have to tell it what we want and prepare ourselves so that we're ready when we get it. It's also important not to put bad things out into the universe. Examples for use in a sentence: "I keep getting hit on by creepy guys—I must be sending out a weird vibe and confusing the universe," or "I feel good about that job interview. I did my best, and now it's up to the universe."

Acknowledgments

From Both of Us:
A million thanks to Dan Mandel, who is the best agent in the universe and also, magically, ours. Thank you to our wonderful manager Brad Petrigala and our film agent Sarah Self for believing in us. We are extremely grateful to Anne Cole, Mary Ellen O'Neill, Shelby Meizlik, Steve Ross, and everyone else at Collins. We know how hard you all worked to bring our baby to life, and we are so appreciative.

There are two very special groups of Hot Chicks that we need to thank. First, thank you so much to all of our girlfriends who talked us through heartache and breakups and confusion and loneliness and basically taught us everything in this book. We couldn't have written this without your wisdom and friendship. We also want to send a huge shout-out to every Hot Chick who read *How to Eat Like a Hot Chick* and e-mailed us to say that it made you feel good, as well as all of you Hot Chicks who picked up this book. We are extremely honored to enter your lives for just a few moments to remind you how special you are and that you deserve all of the goodness in the world. Keep those e-mails coming and remember how hot you are!

From Jodi:
Thank you to my parents for showing me what love, marriage, and a beautiful relationship looks like, and to the rest of my family for their love. I am so lucky to have a wonderful second family that has welcomed me with loving open arms, so thank you to all of the Heaps for that. For inspiring this material, supporting me on my way to finding love, and/or just being a great friend, I thank

Robin Fineman, Kathleen Black, and the much-missed and loved Sherie Beth Weinstein. Cerina, thank you for doing for me all of the things that we both hope this book will do for the women who read it. And finally, thank you Dan for giving me your love.

From Cerina:

Mom, thank you for being an example of unconditional love. You're a true Hot Chick and I hope to replicate such genuine devotion in my own life. Dad, thank you for your loving encouragement and thoughtful advice on love—they have made me a better partner and I lovingly cherish that. Gino and Angela, thank you for making me feel that the bond between siblings is one of the most special loves on the planet. Courtney and Karen, thank you for keeping me strong in times of confusion, and for reminding me that sometimes you have to "fight for love"—I'm forever grateful. Thank you Libby for giving me a crash course in "Libby School." Your words guided me to a new, more loving, confident path in life. Thank you Jodi, the greatest business partner in the universe♥. I'm blessed to have your loving friendship, and the experience of celebrating our heyday♥ together, as we guided each other to finding our true loves. And finally, thank you to my lover, my best friend, and my partner for eternity. Benjamin, darling, thank you for loving me and making me your wife; it's because of you that I know what true love is.